From the Inside-Out

From the Inside-Out

Concrete Steps to Transforming Education Today

Richard A. Andrusiak, Amanda Bastoni,
Carlton J. Fitzgerald, Christopher Geraghty,
Simona Laurian-Fitzgerald,
and Ruthann Petruno-Goguen

ROWMAN & LITTLEFIELD
Lanham • Boulder • New York • London

Published by Rowman & Littlefield
An imprint of The Rowman & Littlefield Publishing Group, Inc.
4501 Forbes Boulevard, Suite 200, Lanham, Maryland 20706
www.rowman.com
6 Tinworth Street, London SE11 5AL, United Kingdom

Copyright © 2020 Richard A. Andrusiak, Amanda Bastoni, Carlton J. Fitzgerald, Christopher Geraghty, Simona Laurian-Fitzgerald, and Ruthann Petruno-Goguen

All rights reserved. No part of this book may be reproduced in any form or by any electronic or mechanical means, including information storage and retrieval systems, without written permission from the publisher, except by a reviewer who may quote passages in a review.

British Library Cataloguing in Publication Information Available

Library of Congress Cataloging-in-Publication Data
Names: Andrusiak, Rich, 1974– author.
Title: From the inside-out : concrete steps to transforming education today / Rich Andrusiak, Amanda Bastoni, Carlton J. Fitzgerald, Christopher Geraghty, and Ruthann Petruno-Goguen.
Description: Lanham, Maryland : Rowman & Littlefield Publishers, 2020. | Includes bibliographical references. | Summary: "Schools need to dramatically reform and educators need to lead the way"— Provided by publisher.
Identifiers: LCCN 2020007306 | ISBN 9781475853766 (cloth) | ISBN 9781475853773 (paperback) | ISBN 9781475853780 (epub)
Subjects: LCSH: Educational change—United States. | Education—Aims and objectives—United States. | Teachers—Professional relationships—United States. | Individualized instruction—United States.
Classification: LCC LA217.2 .A55 2020 | DDC 370.973—dc23
LC record available at https://lccn.loc.gov/2020007306

To our past, present, and future students.

Contents

Foreword by Gavin Henning		ix
Preface		xi
Introduction		xiii
1	Reform Before It Is Too Late *Carlton J. Fitzgerald and Simona Laurian-Fitzgerald*	1
2	A Call for Change From Within the Classroom *Christopher Geraghty*	21
3	Eliminating Exams From Gateway College Mathematics Courses: Going beyond Corequisite Mathematics *Richard A. Andrusiak*	41
4	Every Child Must Be Valued *Amanda Bastoni*	71
5	Challenging *Status Quo* From One Superintendent's Perspective *Ruthann Petruno-Goguen*	91
6	What Next: Boom or Bust *Carlton J. Fitzgerald and Simona Laurian-Fitzgerald*	123
References		151
About the Authors		163

Foreword

I have the best job in the world. As a professor and program director, I get to do what I love—learn—in all aspects of my position—whether this is keeping abreast of new issues and developments in higher education, revising and creating courses, or serving on dissertation committees. Another great part of my job is working with remarkable students and faculty who are talented and committed educators.

The New England College former doctoral students and faculty who wrote this book continue to teach me through their insightful analysis of educational reform. All readers of this book, regardless of their role in education, will take something new away from the chapters—something that can concretely and immediately be applied to their own educational context.

The authors begin with the premise that the U.S. primary and secondary education system is broken. Developed to prepare students to work in society created by the Industrial Revolution, the system is woefully outdated. The goal of the current system is still to create standardized copies of rule-abiding, mechanistic students. As the authors skillfully note, this one-size-fits-all, rigid system of education does not meet the current or future needs of a global society, and this system is not attentive to the rich diversity of students attending schools today.

In a world of assembly line robots, self-check registers, and artificial intelligence that can be held in our hand, no longer needed are graduates who can complete simple tasks. What is needed are individuals who can think critically, solve problems, work collaboratively, and communicate effectively in all media. The authors emphatically proclaim that our schools are not teaching our students these vital skills and as such are failing both society and students.

They argue that what is needed to address these shortcomings is education reform coming from inside the system driven by teachers. Leading this reform must be a future-thinking vision for primary and secondary education—one that is attentive to job skills for information and gig economies, but one that also views education beyond simply job training and centers schooling on human development.

This vision challenges the *status quo* and acknowledges, embraces, and leverages the diversity of students in all forms. Success looks different when the educational system views each student as unique, with their own distinctive talents, experiences, and needs. In this system of education re-visioned by the authors, every single student is valued.

The student who aspires to be a rocket scientist is appreciated the same as one who strives to be an electrician as each of these careers is critical for our society. Teaching is personalized, yet universal so that all students are included and benefitted. All students grow and develop. No students are left behind.

This vision may seem idyllic and unrealistic. Change is difficult and not easy for entrenched societal institutions such as education. The authors provide concrete, actionable steps that can be taken to realize this vision. Educational revolution and evolution is possible when started within by valuing the voices of all teachers and empowering them to actualize their voices.

Students are vital partners in their own learning and educational change. Through an equitable and inclusive student-centered approach to teaching and learning, the educational system in the United States can be transformed to meet the needs of today and prepare students to be the problem solvers of tomorrow.

Gavin Henning
New England College

Gavin Henning is a professor of Higher Education and the director of the Doctorate of Education and Master of Science in Higher Education Administration programs at New England College. Prior to becoming a full-time faculty member, Gavin spent twenty years in higher education administration working in residence life, institutional research, and student affairs assessment.

Preface

Most people agree that the future will require different skills than were necessary for the past, and twenty years into the twenty-first century, people are still talking about twenty-first-century skills. People like Kai-Fu Lee (2018), David Sousa (2017), Tony Wagner (2016), and Sir Ken Robinson (2017) have discussed from different perspectives that we should be teaching different skills in different ways than many schools do presently. The purpose of this book is to provide concrete actionable steps that educators can begin today to transform education to meet the future needs of our students.

As we look at the cultural, economic, technological, and social changes in our world, we know that our future students will be entering very different environments in their places of work, in their communities, and in the world. Jobs are already being lost to technology, and Lee (2018) explains that many, if not most, low-skill and medium-skill jobs will no longer exist. The advent of artificial intelligence is quickly changing our world. Educational institutions must transform to maintain relevancy and meet the future needs of our students.

According to Calum McClelland (2018), a two-year study conducted by the McKinsey Global Institute predicts, by 2030, artificial intelligence will replace up to 30 percent of the world's human labor force. That would mean replacing approximately 800 million people. If American schools continue to educate our students from an Industrial Revolution mentality, the present authors believe that will be setting students up for failure. Though we know not what many jobs of the future will be, we do know that flexibility, creativity, collaboration, and the ability to understand diversity will play integral roles in our world.

Our society will not be able to afford to have students fail or be undereducated in our schools. All of our students will have to become independent lifelong learners. If we continue to educate our students as if they will be living in the past (or even the present), we will fail them. Our students deserve better.

This book is our attempt to add our voices and ideas to those who are inspiring us to speak out for the future education of our nation and world. This book discusses important future educational issues and presents actionable steps for transforming education, from the perspectives of a Career and Technical Education director, a college mathematics professor, a school superintendent, a high school social studies teacher, a literature professor, and a former public school teacher, principal, associate professor, and associate dean of education.

The future is here, and educators must respond accordingly. If schools continue to ignore the realities of the future, more and more students will graduate unprepared for their future lives. Pretending that everything will somehow work out on its own is immoral. Educators must take over education before it is too late. Schools need to be transformed, not reformed. And, the present authors assert, the transformation must happen *From the Inside-Out*.

Introduction

This book is organized into six chapters, with each chapter written from a different perspective: a public school and college teacher and administrator; a university professor of literature and pedagogy; a high school teacher and department chair of the social studies; a community college professor and former department of education coordinator of mathematics; a Career and Technical Education (CTE) director; and a superintendent of schools. The authors developed their ideas based on the following assumptions:

1. Our educational systems must be transformed.
2. That transformation should be led by educators.
3. Each student must be valued in every school and in every classroom.
4. Success looks different for each student.

From these common assumptions, each author discusses the important aspects of the future of education. The premise is that educational transformation must occur now, before it is too late. The future is already here, and educators are still discussing what to do about it. Despite many good-intentioned efforts, too little has changed. Educators must do the right thing for students and take back control of the educational process so that students will be at the center of the teaching and learning process.

This book is important to do now because we are approaching a point of no return in our educational systems. At some point, soon, it will become too late, and our educational systems, as we know them, will crash. That is exactly what some people want, the destruction of public education. If that occurs, it will be disastrous for millions of students all around the world. It will weaken the democratic process and widen the gaps among the haves and the have-nots. Students and teachers are yearning to work in a system of education that will help them become excited about school. This book contributes to that transformational process.

To accomplish those goals, this book progresses through six perspectives to help readers understand the thought processes of the authors through six elements of the inside-out transformational process. Each element has been developed so that different educators can find themselves in multiple areas of the book.

First, readers will review different ideas about the core premise of the book—to transform education, all educators must accept the philosophy that education must be student-centered (see chapter 1). All students must be successful in school, if they are going to be prepared for their future lives. Understanding and celebrating diversity are essential elements of student-centered teaching and learning, and this understanding undergirds the rest of the book.

Second, the interactions and power structure between and among teachers and students must change (see chapter 2). Teachers and students must become partners in the educational process. Educators and students must go beyond student voice and choice to develop interdependent responsibilities for teaching and learning. For inside-out transformation to occur, teachers and students must take co-responsibility for teaching and learning. The teaching and learning process must move from hierarchical to collegial. In a coleadership process, teachers and students are responsible to be leaders and learners.

Third, how teachers teach and how students are assessed must transform (see chapter 3). Creating student-centered open projects in which students are working on important student-developed questions or problems, based on their work and/or interests, is central to helping students move from dependent learners to independent learners. Assessments must be real-world assessments, codeveloped and coimplemented by students and their instructors. Traditional forms of summative assessments must be replaced by more authentic and real-world connected assessments.

Fourth, in a student-centered educational world, schools and all educational programs will function to create systems that benefit all students, not individual schools or programs (see chapter 4). Recommendations for student programming must be developed for the best interests of students and not in the best interest of individual schools or programs. Interactions among different schools (e.g., traditional high schools and CTE schools) must be cooperative, not competitive. Programming for students must be equitable and assessed in relation to student wants and needs and not on the reputation of any specific school or program.

Fifth, how schools, principals, and teachers develop professionally, and how they are assessed must be transformed (see chapters 5 and 6). Superintendents must challenge the *status quo* and change the philosophies, policies, mission statements, and practices that interfere with student-centered teaching and learning. *Status quo* is failing our students and teachers, and superintendents (and boards of education) must develop the courage and insight to do what is right for students.

Finally, teachers must have ways to enter into student-centered teaching and learning practices, and administrators must have assessment practices that support teachers in their efforts (see chapter 6). School boards and their communities must support professional development for their teachers and principals. *Status quo* is not acceptable, and it is time for teachers, students, and principals to put education where it belongs, in the hands of teachers and students.

This book gives educators a philosophy of education for the future. The time to implement such a system is now and not later. One book cannot answer all of the questions or give all of the ingredients to create the system for the future. This book, though, does give educators concrete ideas and techniques to move forward in the process. If each superintendent, principal, and teacher takes one or more ideas from this book, they will transform education. They just might change their school; that might help change their district; that might help other districts change; that might change their state; and who knows, that might change education.

Chapter 1

Reform Before It Is Too Late

Carlton J. Fitzgerald and Simona Laurian-Fitzgerald

Twenty years into the twenty-first century, educators, politicians, and the public are still discussing what and how to help teachers prepare students for their futures. A small group of educators who work in varied positions, and who come from different perspectives (i.e., Career and Technical Education [CTE] director, college professors, school superintendent, high school teacher, former public school principal, and associate dean of education) has decided to move much more quickly, or it will be too late for teachers and students.

Ken Robinson (2017) explains that he believes schools have the complex role of helping students be economically, socially, culturally, and personally prepared for their lives after graduation from high school or college/university. Schools were developed for a time that was different than today, and certainly different than the future.

Kai-Fu Lee (2019), in his discussions about the role of artificial intelligence for the future of students, explores the possibility that many of the jobs that exist today will disappear. People are already seeing jobs disappearing in manufacturing and transportation, and, according to Lee, workers potentially will see most nonskilled, semiskilled, and even more sophisticated jobs being taken over by robots or other forms of artificial intelligence.

Paul Romer (2016), a 2018 Nobel Prize winner in economics, has developed the concept of conditional optimism. Citizens face many obstacles in the future of our nation and the world, and the idea that people do not have to worry, because things always fall into place, is dangerous thinking. If society stands by and just hopes for the best, it could result in economic chaos in America and all over the world.

According to conditional optimism, there are appropriate ways to deal with these issues through educational development, economic policies, and the political will to make the changes necessary to create an optimistic future. Doing nothing and hoping for the best will lead to failure. Hoping for a better future for teachers and students will not accomplish the goals necessary for transforming the educational process in the United States or any other nation. Educators must transform education now.

What should be changed in educational systems? The first issue to address is the notion that our schools cannot be reformed into the future, they must be transformed. Education, as it is presently organized and run, continues, for the most part, to produce followers and compliers (Preble & Gordan, 2011). Despite the failures of the accountability mentality (Ravitch, 2016), education continues to foster convergent thinking and skill development, rather than divergent thinking and skill development.

People like Aoun (2017) and Davidson (2017) agree that our schools were developed for another time (i.e., the Industrial Revolution). Times have changed, society has changed, technology has changed, communication has changed, the world economy has changed, national and world politics have changed, but schools, including colleges and universities, have essentially not changed.

Davidson (2017) writes:

> Space travel. The metaphor is evocative, and useful. There has been a before and after that most of my students today don't comprehend, which also means they don't fully grasp how unprepared the outmoded educational systems have left them in this world. (p. 6)

The authors of this book agree and believe educators, politicians, and the public should change assumptions about education, and then based on those assumptions, change what is taught, how it is taught, how teachers work with students, and how educators assess themselves and their students, before it is too late. Teachers and parents do not fully understand how unprepared our educational system is leaving students, and, if we fail to act, our students will not be prepared for life after graduation.

Students are preparing to live in a world of revolutionary changes, and education is charged with adapting how schools prepare our students. Teachers must think differently about the skills and talents of students. Schools must be run differently, or they will fail our students. Thus, this book has been created based on the following assumptions:

1. Our educational systems must be transformed.
2. That transformation should be led by educators.
3. Each student must be valued in every school and in every classroom.
4. Success looks different for each student.

EDUCATION MUST BE TRANSFORMED

Tony Wagner, in his 2014 book, *The global achievement gap: Why even our best schools don't teach the new survival skills our children need—and what we can do about it*, discusses his interviews with top businesspeople around the world, and what CEOs see as missing from their young workers in the field. From his analysis of his interviews, Wagner has developed what he calls the seven survival skills that students need to be successful in their future careers. His survival skills include:

1. critical thinking and problem-solving,
2. collaboration across networks and leading by influence,
3. agility and adaptability,
4. initiative and entrepreneurialism,
5. effective oral and written communication,
6. accessing and analyzing information, and
7. curiosity and imagination.

Ken Robinson (2017) adds:

When I talk with business leaders, they complain that education isn't producing the people they urgently need: people who are literate, numerate, who can analyze information and ideas; who can generate new ideas and implement them; who can communicate clearly and work well with other people. (p. 6)

Educators are charged with creating educated citizens. Students need to be prepared to be effective and positive citizens and workers in a more complex world. Learning curriculum is important, but it is far from sufficient to prepare students for the future. Businesspeople are begging for young people who are intelligent, innovative, and creative. They want workers who are independent and trustworthy, who can solve problems in creative ways, and who understand how to work collaboratively in teams.

Unfortunately, many current educational practices have been so focused on content that many educators have forgotten about the myriad of abilities, talents, and creative potential of too many students. Teachers are not deliberately wasting student talent, but the system is causing them to focus on a narrow set of skills that overlooks and stifles creativity in an enormous number of students. Knowing important concepts and facts is important, but those concepts and facts that are traditionally taught should not be the only curricula available for our students.

Political and educational leaders have determined that every student should learn the exact same things, in the exact same way, and be assessed by a single assessment tool. That focus has caused schools to remain in the mindset of the Industrial Revolution. Laurian-Fitzgerald, Popa, and Fitzgerald (2015) have found that students want more than a canned education riddled with teacher-proof curricula. Students want to be engaged in active, thoughtful, and thought-provoking work.

Christopher Geraghty (chapter 2) has found that many students and teachers are discouraged with the education in which they are involved. Teachers indicate they want to teach more effectively, and students indicate they want to learn more important and relevant knowledge and skills. The present authors believe students and teachers are stuck in a system that will never give them what they want and need. The system is broken, not the students, teachers, or principals, and, until the system is changed, students and educators will continue to be frustrated and discouraged. They all deserve better.

In this book, the authors question the established assumptions, because they agree that schools should work to help all students find their interests, passions, talents, and skills to reach their potentials. Ruthann Petruno-Goguen (chapter 5) explains that schools continue to miss the mark when it comes to educating all students. Schools, for the most part, have not effectively addressed achievement gaps, the effects of trauma, the different interests, talents and abilities of students, or the reality of poverty and its effects on students.

The present authors also believe being prepared for the world of work is but one important aspect of a great education. Students will be much more than workers; they will also be the next generation of parents, politicians, intellectuals, artists, environmentalists, religious leaders, and inventors. Students need assistance to find their talents and passions to create positive mindsets, so they will enrich our world with intelligence, creativity, and care.

The world is changing rapidly. Our students will be living in a very different world from the one that our educational system was developed to send them. Clearly, a significant percentage of our graduates will be working in jobs that have not yet been invented. Workers in the future will probably have to change careers numerous times during their working years.

Schools will have to help students develop skills to be flexible and innovative, so they will have the ability to navigate changes in the economic, social, cultural, and political systems. According to Hammond (2015), cultural awareness and competence is already important, and she believes its importance will continue to grow.

Our students will most likely be working in an international economic system that will require collaborative skills and cultural competence, if they are going to be successful in the future. Many more graduates will be in careers in which they will be working in teams where they will have to cooperate, collaborate, problem-solve, and develop creative solutions to unique and complex issues that will arise in their future organizations.

Schools need to develop leaders, enhance curiosity and creativity, assist students in finding their passions, engage every student in complex and deep learning, and move students from dependent learners to lifelong independent learners. The kinds of changes being discussed here cannot be accomplished by simply adjusting the present educational system. The present educational system must be replaced by a more student-centered process, based on the following assumptions.

1. Every student must be successful in school, meaning every student has to learn effectively and gain the kinds of skills necessary for success in life: critical thinking, problem-solving, communication, cooperation and collaboration, creative thinking, flexibility, and entrepreneurship, all based on a paradigm of diversity and cultural understandings.
2. Every human being is important, and schools can no longer afford to waste the diverse talents and skills of their students.
3. Education is about helping diverse students develop their individual talents and skills to reach their potentials.
4. Teaching and learning must be student-centered.

STUDENT-CENTERED EDUCATION

The third and fourth assumptions upon which this book is based are as follows: Each student must be valued in every school and in every classroom, and success looks different for each student. If educators are going to develop a system that will connect with these assumptions, then it is abundantly clear that assumptions about education must change. The following three assumptions should be replaced:

1. For good teaching and learning to occur in our schools, society must hold students, teachers, and principals accountable.
2. The major goal of public education is to ensure that all students learn the same things and prove what they know in the same way (e.g., standardized tests and common assessments).
3. The role of teachers is to control what is learned, when it is learned, and how it is learned.

When educators are brainwashed into believing the main goal of education is accountability, then test scores become more important than students. This mentality causes principals and teachers to narrow the curriculum to what is tested. The authors of this book have witnessed firsthand how fearful teachers and principals become with high-stakes tests. So, they naturally teach to those tests and leave out other important experiences that students should have in school. According to Ravitch (2016), the public is given the illusion that test scores relate to high standards, when there is very little evidence to back up those claims.

When schools narrow the curriculum because educators have been ordered to believe everyone should learn the same things and develop the same skills, the talents and potentials of our students are limited. That process also limits the creativity and talents of teachers. Instead, schools should be encouraging and supporting students to learn more, not less. Educators should not limit creativity, rather they should encourage creativity.

Davidson (2017) points out:

> Students need new ways of integrating knowledge, including through reflection on why and what they are learning. They don't need more "teaching to the test." They need to be offered challenges that promote their success after graduation, when all the educational testing has stopped. This is an engaged form of student-centered pedagogy known as "active learning." (p. 8)

Limiting what teachers and students do to a list of curricula goals is nowhere near sufficient for the future success of students.

What Is Student-Centered Learning?

According to the Coalition of Essential Schools (n.d.), student-centered teaching and learning can be defined as follows:

> Student-Centered Teaching and Learning focuses on the needs, abilities, interests, and learning styles of the students and has many implications for the design of curriculum, course content, and interactivity of courses. Accordingly, a prominent pedagogy will be teacher-as-coach, to provoke students to learn how to learn and thus to teach themselves, rather than the more traditional teacher-centered learning with teacher-as-deliverer-of-instructional-services, which places the teacher at its center in an active role and students in a passive, receptive role. This pedagogy acknowledges student voice as central to the learning experience for every learner and requires students to be active, responsible participants in their own learning. To capitalize on this, teaching and learning should be personalized to the maximum feasible extent. Decisions about the details of the course of study, the use of students' and teachers' time, and the choice of teaching materials and specific pedagogies must be unreservedly placed in the hands of the staff and students. (p. 1)

This process is a collaboration among teachers and students, where the goal is to move the students into the role of leader for their education in partnership with a professional educator. The shifting of power from outside of the classroom to inside the classroom must occur, so students and their teachers can work together freely to develop important student goals and experiences.

Habits of Mind

In order for teaching and learning to be student-centered, students have to develop skills to help them become more independent learners. Richard Andrusiak (chapter 3) discusses the habits of mind students must have to become critical thinkers. He explains how the habits of mind are important for students to develop as they take over more of their own education. Costa and Kallick (2008) created sixteen habits of mind related to critical thinking to help teachers in their work with their students. Their habits include:

1. persisting,
2. managing impulsivity,
3. listening with understanding and empathy,
4. thinking flexibly,
5. thinking about thinking (metacognition),
6. striving for accuracy,
7. questioning and posing problems,
8. applying past knowledge to new situations,
9. thinking and communicating with clarity and precision,
10. gathering data through all senses,
11. creating, imagining, innovating,
12. responding with wonderment and awe,
13. taking responsible risks,
14. finding humor,
15. thinking interdependently, and
16. remaining open to continuous learning.

The Foundation and Center for Critical Thinking (2017) also developed concepts of critical-thinking habits for students and teachers. The foundation and center have developed a strategy list of thirty-five critical-thinking skills for teachers to use with their students. They break the skills into affective skills, macro skills, and micro skills. Their nine affective strategies help teachers develop critical-thinking attitudes and habits that will help students grow as independent and critical thinkers. The nine affective skills include:

1. thinking independently,
2. developing insight into egocentricity or sociocentricity,
3. exercising fairmindedness,

4. exploring thoughts underlying feelings and feelings underlying thoughts,
5. developing intellectual humility and suspending judgment,
6. developing intellectual courage,
7. developing intellectual good faith and integrity,
8. developing intellectual perseverance, and
9. developing confidence in reason.

These affective skills, attitudes, and habits are developed over time as teachers set up experiences for students to rehearse and practice these skills, receive effective feedback and advice, and move to higher skill levels. If students develop and integrate these affective skills and habits into their work at school, upon graduation, they will be prepared for their journey beyond graduation.

How can teachers control the curriculum to a set, designated list of objectives and help students master their habits of mind? It is impossible to integrate these habits in meaningful ways, if teachers believe that the set of curriculum objectives is more important than the human growth of their students. Students do not develop these habits in the one project they do in November. Habits are formed by consistently and creatively connecting learning to the student and to the real world. Students have to be engaged in complex experiences that encourage them to work hard, persist in their endeavors, collaborate with their peers, and think critically.

Instead of a convergent curriculum, students need divergent curricula and exposure to a vast array of experiences. Critical thinking becomes habit only if students are nourished throughout their educational career. Caine (2018) and Caine (2011) offer that students have to be responsible for their learning, so they will be fully engaged and focused on their own growth, with the school encouraging and assisting students all along the journey. Students, in other words, have to be at the center of the learning process (e.g., not test scores, not teachers, not politicians, not curriculum).

Student-Centered Assumptions and Beliefs

According to Lea, Stephenson, and Troy (2003), successful student-centered teaching and learning experiences should be based on the following tenets:

1. a reliance on active rather than passive learning experiences,
2. an emphasis on deep learning and understanding,
3. an increase in student responsibility and authority,
4. an increase in student autonomy,
5. an interdependence between the teacher and the learner,
6. mutual respect for the teacher and learner relationship, and
7. a reflexive approach to teaching and learning on the part of the teacher and the learner.

From their research, Fitzgerald-Laurian, Popa, and Fitzgerald (2015) developed a philosophical overview for student-centered teaching and learning. They developed sixteen philosophical pillars for student-centered learning that they have turned into the following philosophical action goals:

In our classrooms all students will:

1. be successful learners;
2. be actively engaged in their learning;
3. make as many choices as possible in their learning;
4. work positively and regularly with other students in a variety of ways;
5. be encouraged to be curious;
6. do meaningful work most of the time they are in school;
7. work on complex projects both individually and in teams;
8. become independent workers, as well as good teammates;
9. integrate the arts as an important part of their learning experiences;
10. set goals for their learning;
11. be supported to take intelligent risks in their learning;
12. understand that learning depends on great strategic efforts;
13. understand their place in the world;
14. develop fair-mindedness, empathy, and understanding in their work with and about other people;
15. be supported in their efforts socially and academically by their peers and by their teacher; and
16. work in a positive and supportive class environment.

If students are placed into the center of the teaching and learning process and reach these goals, they will have educational experiences that will foster their growth socially, psychologically, culturally, and educationally (Johnson & Johnson, 2013; Laurian-Fitzgerald & Fitzgerald, 2016). The good news is that all of these actions are present in many schools, and the goal is to keep the process moving and growing. The hope is that the present book will help move the process along more rapidly, since we are already 20 percent of the way through the twenty-first century.

Student-Centered Elements

Laurian-Fitzgerald and Fitzgerald (2018) developed ten elements for instructors to consider when attempting to create student-centered educational experiences. Their student-centered elements include:

1. constructivist activities,
2. metacognitive reflections,
3. student and professor partnerships,

4. collaborative/cooperative efforts,
5. authentic assessments,
6. active and ongoing student engagement in the work to learn,
7. explicit teaching of important skills,
8. student control of at least some of their learning,
9. peer and professor/teacher feedback, and
10. learning based, to a large extent, on student effort.

In their work with undergraduate pre-service teachers, Laurian-Fitzgerald and Fitzgerald (2018) found, after implementing the ten student-centered elements, students were more engaged, worked harder, collaborated more effectively, and achieved more than did colleagues in previous versions of the same class. Students also self-reported they felt they and their instructor worked harder and more effectively than in other classes. One student wrote, "Professors should use these kinds of techniques in all of our classes" (p. 6). The professor in this study reported, "The students were so much more engaged this term. They came to class more prepared, and they were enthusiastic about their learning. That encouraged me to be even more creative for them. They made me become a better teacher" (p. 7).

Niche Construction

Armstrong (2012) uses the term niche construction to describe his version of student-centeredness. He believes all the neural diversity found in classes is normal; it is the natural state of the world. Instead of looking at students who are different as being handicapped, Armstrong believes we should look at all students as being differently abled, and educators should construct learning experiences based on student strengths, not on weaknesses or deficits.

Every person has a niche upon which teachers can build to help students enhance their knowledge and skills. If teachers learn how to employ the strengths, interests, and passions of every student, then students will learn more deeply and remember what they learned more effectively.

Caine (2018) reinforces the concept of niche construction in his discussions about teaching to the natural learning structures of student brains. Caine et al. (2016) believe students should be given the responsibility and the authority to lead their own educational journeys. In other words, education should be student-centered.

Caine et al. (2016) discuss three tiers of teaching in which instructors and students move from curriculum-centered and teacher-centered processes (tier 1), to more student-centered processes (tier 2), and to completely student-centered processes (tier 3). Students, according to this system, should be involved in complex learning experiences in which students expand their creative, problem-solving, and critical-thinking abilities by working on self-designed real-world issues. Teacher roles change in each tier, as the instructor moves from developing the learning to becoming a mentor for their students, as the students develop their own learning experiences.

Student-Centered Questions

Student-centered teaching and learning require educators to ask different questions. What questions are asked and how they are asked matter a great deal. If teachers create mediocre questions, then they will receive mediocre answers. For example, if a school district asks a question like, "How can we hold teachers and principals accountable?" then they will only gather accountability responses. Instead, if the district asks a question like, "How can we help all students feel important, find their passions and voices, and reach their potentials?" then teachers will create very different answers. Instead of making every student pass the same test (the answer to the accountability question), we might begin by reviewing the elements for student-centered teaching and learning to create very different educational experiences. Teachers will develop very different questions similar to those displayed in table 1.1.

Table 1.1 **Student-Centered Educator Questions**

Student-Centered Elements	Educator Questions
1. Constructivist activities	What prerequisite skills and knowledge do my students need to be successful in their present learning?
2. Metacognitive reflections	How can I help my students think about how they learn best in different situations?
3. Student and professor partnerships	How do I find out about my students' interests and passions? How can I use that information to help my students learn?
4. Collaborative/cooperative efforts	What kinds of collaborative skills do my students need now to be effective team members?
5. Authentic assessments	How can I help students to develop assessments that are connected to their interests, passions, and the real world?
6. Active and ongoing student engagement	How can I hook every student to this unit of study?
7. Explicit teaching of important skills	How can I assess student needs for the skills of this learning unit? How can I teach the needed skills to the students who need them?
8. Students' control of their learning	What students are ready to take on more authority for their learning?
9. Peer and professor/teacher feedback	Have I developed appropriate peer, self, and teacher assessments and feedback for this unit of study?
10. Learning based on strategic student effort	Am I giving each student the feedback and follow-up experiences to effectively learn the present material and skills?

These are just samples of the kinds of questions instructors might ask. Principals would ask some different questions, as would curriculum coordinators and superintendents. The point is if educators ask student-centered questions, then they and their students will create student-centered responses that will more likely lead to the development of experiences with and for students, based on their needs, wants, interests, and passions.

The answers to these questions will also allow educators to develop different roles as teachers to assist students to develop in their ability to move from dependent to independent learners, compliers to leaders, responders to inquirers, receivers of knowledge to creators of knowledge, and supervisees in the learning process to supervisors of their own learning.

Naturally, as teachers move from the professor of information and knowledge to mentor to adviser to partner of learning, this means a shift in the roles of teachers and administrators. This will take time, and teachers and principals will need assistance to learn and adjust to the different levels of understanding for their different roles. But educators know how to learn and, as our students take more and more control for and of their learning, teachers will be excited and proud to be part of their journeys.

Own Their Learning

It is essential that students move from dependent learners to independent learners if they are to be prepared to become productive local, national, and international citizens. That means, of course, that teachers and schools have to be willing to scaffold the process with and for their students to effectively take ownership of their learning (Novak, 2016). Student-centered learning can only really become effective if students own their learning. That means students must become fully engaged in the teaching and learning process.

Dewey (1910) advocated for students to be more in charge of their learning many years ago. He believed that almost everything students learned should be directly useful to them in their real worlds. Learning, according to Dewey, should assist all students to reach their goals in life. Caine (2018) believes that the goal should be to have students completely in charge of their learning, and they should use teachers as guides or advisors in the process.

In order to move from dependent to independent learners, Bruner (1961) advocated that students should be discoverers in the learning process. Students, in his view, should work on projects or experiments that they are more and more in charge of creating, in order to find out for themselves what they need to learn. Kolb's (1984) version of a similar process is called inquiry-based learning. In this process the students are inquirers who develop questions, projects, or experiments to assess their ideas and theories. Kraus and Boss (2013) attempt to deepen the thinking in their versions of project-based learning, in which students take more and more control of their learning as they become more independent and more proficient with their critical-thinking skills.

Christopher Geraghty (chapter 2) describes the process of an action research partnership among teachers and students in which the students not only took charge of their learning, but the teachers and students worked together to improve their school for more teachers and students. This process, according to Duckworth (2016), helps students and teachers reach their highest level of passion. When what students do for their own passion becomes something they do for other people, then they reach their highest order of meaningfulness. At this stage they are going beyond themselves into another sphere of meaning and influence. They are making their world a better place.

According to Maslow (1970, 1971) students, who use their talents and skills to help other people, move beyond their basic needs and are approaching self-actualization. They are becoming the persons they want to be (Duckworth, 2016; Fitzgerald & Laurian, 2013). When students experience this kind of learning, they can enter what Csikszentmihalyi (1990; 2008) calls flow—the optimum experience. Robinson (2017) describes flow as an experience when two hours feels like five minutes to a student. When students are that into their learning, they own their work. They are not doing the work for a grade, they are not trying to give their teachers what the teachers want, they are learning for the love of learning.

Meeting Student Physiological and Emotional Needs

To this point the chapter has discussed ways for teachers and schools to help students meet their academic and learning needs. Educators also must understand the importance of emotions in learning (Fitzgerald & Johnson, 2013; Sousa, 2017). This is important, because emotions play a huge role in how people are motivated and choose to behave. From an internal perspective, people behave to meet their internal needs.

Glasser's *Choice theory* (1998) explains that all people do from birth to death is behave to meet genetically based needs for survival, love and belonging, power and accomplishment, fun, and freedom. The present authors add a sixth need to the list—existentialism or meaningfulness.

Maslow (1970, 1971) similarly described human needs as including: physiology, safety, social belonging, self-esteem, self-actualization, and transcendence. When Maslow started his hierarchy of needs, he believed that people did not move to the next level of needs until they had satisfied their needs at the lower level. As time progressed, Maslow revised his thinking to believe people move along different stages throughout life. Maslow (1971) also revised his ideas about self-actualization and added transcendence, giving of oneself to something beyond the self, to his hierarchy.

Table 1.2 Human Needs

Glasser and Fitzgerald and Laurian	Maslow
Existentialism/meaning	Transcendence
Freedom and fun	Self-actualization
	Aesthetic
	Cognitive
Power	Esteem
Love and belonging	Social belonging and love
Survival	Safety physiology

Sources: Fitzgerald and Laurian (2013); Glasser (1998); and Maslow (1970, 1971).

The importance of the works of Glasser (1998) and Maslow (1970, 1971) is the notion that people are motivated by their own needs (see table 1.2). According to this process, almost all behavior is chosen and purposeful, and people spend their lives trying to keep their needs balanced in a way that makes sense to them. If people can keep these needs balanced, their lives usually are happier. When humans do not meet their basic needs, they are usually frustrated and unhappy.

In essence, all people choose behavior to:

a. maintain a sense of control and balance,
b. get more control and balance, or
c. get some control or balance, if they perceive they have none.

An important point to stress here is that this is an evolving theory that is dynamic and changing and has serious implications for how people get along with each other in all types of relationships from intimate and personal to political and cultural.

In schools, if educational leaders can help students and teachers meet their individual needs, their lives will be better, and they will more likely want to participate in school. When educators help people meet their needs, they, in turn, tend to help other people meet their needs. Thus, relationships are more cooperative and positive (Fitzgerald & Laurian, 2013; Johnson & Johnson, 2009).

Internal Needs

All people are given genetic needs at birth and spend their lives trying to keep those needs in balance. Each person meets their needs for survival, love and belonging, power, freedom, fun, and existentialism or meaning in their own way. Although all people have the same kinds of needs, they are met uniquely as each person experiences life. Thus, each person develops their own profile in relationship to the needs fairly early in life, based on each person's genetic makeup and experiences. Glasser (1998) believed that once our basic profile develops, it does not change much, but what do change are the circumstances in which we live.

Survival (physiology and safety) is the need to be able to live physically and emotionally safe lives (Fitzgerald & Laurian, 2013; Glasser, 1998; Maslow, 1970). Of course, all people have the basic physical needs for food, air, drink, clothing, and shelter. It is very difficult to concentrate on other things if people are always hungry, cold, or physically threatened. Survival also includes the desire for sex that helps ensure the continuation of the species. For some people, the carrying on of the name is an important survival need. For example, family business names are used by some as a way to leave a legacy to survive past death. Many presidents work hard to leave a legacy of their presidencies after they leave office. Another aspect of survival includes people's perceptions of money. Many people say something like: "We have to be able to pay the bills before we can think of spending money on anything else." The need to survive physically is important to people.

Everyone also has emotional survival needs. People need to feel safe emotionally, as well as physically. When people threaten or coerce others, those habits kill emotional support for people. Glasser (1998) called those kinds of behaviors the Deadly Habits. When people feel unsafe emotionally, they feel out of control in their lives. People who are afraid for their emotional safety find it very difficult to concentrate on other things (Sousa, 2017). For example, it is very difficult for students to learn new material when they are fearful of taking a risk in class, because other students may ridicule them.

It is tremendously difficult to be happy when people feel emotionally unsafe. That is why it is so important in schools for teachers to do everything they can to be supportive of their students and to have students be supportive of each other. The same is true in any relationship. People sharing a relationship should do everything possible to be sure that the other(s) in the relationship feels safe, secure, and supported emotionally (Fitzgerald & Laurian, 2013).

The second need is *love and belonging (social belonging and love)*. From a practical perspective, since people live their entire lives meeting (or not meeting) their needs in relationships, this may be the most important need. Every human being needs at least one important relationship in their life to be happy (Fitzgerald & Laurian, 2013; Glasser, 1998; Maslow, 1970, 1971). There are many studies that show the negative effects of the lack of love and care in people's lives. Researchers have found, for example, in orphanages after World War II that babies even died without enough love and attention, even if they were warm and fed (Frankl, 2006).

Love and belonging needs can be met in relationships with individuals, clubs, organizations, and/or work. Love and belonging seems to contain two components. First is the need to be loved by or cared about by others. The second component is the ability to love and care about others. For example, older people who live on their own and have pets actually live longer than people who just live by themselves. A life without love and belonging is a very unfulfilling life. It would be almost impossible to have a balanced and happy life without some love and belonging in it.

Power (*esteem*) is the third internal need (Fitzgerald & Laurian, 2013; Glasser, 1998; Maslow, 1970, 1971). We can define power as the ability to be good at something, to have an influence with people, to have control of some things in life, or to accomplish good things. When people feel powerless, they have to attempt to gain some power or control. This can take very negative forms at times. These people are called "control freaks" or egotistical. They try to have power over others, rather than have power within their own lives.

All people need to feel competent, worthy, and influential. When people perceive that nobody listens to them or their voice does not matter, they will not feel very powerful. In order to be in balance, people need to be able to meet the need for power (self-esteem).

The fourth need is *freedom* (*self-actualization*) (Fitzgerald & Laurian, 2013; Glasser, 1998; Maslow 1970, 1971). Every person needs to be able to make important decisions for themselves. Even in circumstances that inhibit freedom, people need to be able to make decisions for themselves. During World War II, many people who found themselves in concentration camps survived by creating ways to find freedom, even if only in their minds (Frankl, 2006).

People often will do things they know are bad for them, if it means they can make their own decisions. Thousands of kids choose to smoke, vape, or do drugs knowing they are endangering themselves. The freedom of choice, though, is so strong for many of these young people that they choose to do things they know are dangerous. In relationships, when people try to inhibit freedom, they cause problems for the people around them (and for themselves). All people need to be free to make important decisions for themselves.

The fifth need is *fun* (Fitzgerald & Laurian, 2013; Glasser, 1998). Fun is also a part of Maslow's (1971) *self-actualization* need. Freedom and fun are important aspects of how individuals develop into the people they want to be. Glasser actually defined fun as learning. Everyone needs fun in their life on a regular basis. Fun is not a trivial wish that people get if they have some extra time.

Children seem to understand this intuitively. They are going to have fun as often as they can. Adults often seem to believe that fun is not a need but a fringe benefit they can sometimes have and sometimes not have. All work and no play not only makes Jack a dull boy, it makes Jack less self-actualized and more unbalanced and unhappy. It is important for adults to choose to have fun in their lives. In education some people call this lifelong learning. When people stop learning, they stop growing into the people they want to be. If people have a hard time remembering the last time they had fun, it is time to schedule some fun in their life. Everyone deserves it, and all people need it.

The final need is *existentialism or meaningfulness (transcendence)* (Fitzgerald & Laurian, 2013; Maslow, 1971). This need can be defined as being part of something bigger than oneself. Frankl (2006) talks about finding a "reason for being." Each person needs to find their purpose or meaning in life. Once a person finds their meaning, they can follow a path to realize their purpose in our universe.

This notion is the idea of selflessness of purpose. Here the belief is that real happiness is not found in the receiving but is rather found in the giving. Norton (2012) talks about how people who give or do things for others are happier than people who do not. The famous playwright, Henry Miller, reportedly once said something like, "If there is peace in this world, it is not in having, but it is in being." People do not become fulfilled and happy by getting love, but by being loving, not in gaining power but by empowering, not in getting fun but in being joyful, and not in gaining meaning but in creating meaning.

In this view, the more people give, the more balanced they become. To have a loving relationship, people should act lovingly, or give love. In return, the more they share their love with others, the more love they usually receive. The same is true of all of the needs. The way to a balanced life is to do meaningful things with and for others and to allow them to do the same with us.

This author remembers one evening viewing the Johnny Carson show, a late-night comedy show. In his monologue, Johnny was joking about one of his guests, Mr. Rogers, and his audience was laughing at the thought of Mr. Rogers, a minister and children's TV show personality, trying to deal with the slick comedian. Within five minutes of talking with Johnny, Mr. Rogers had Johnny eating out of his hands. His loving and selfless personhood was no match, and this author watched how Johnny was transformed by being with Mr. Rogers. In school the more teachers and principals help students become more of whom they are supposed to be, the more educators become whom they are supposed to be.

CONCLUSIONS

There is a saying that some people say came from a gravestone in England that helps to begin to answer the question: Where do I begin? The saying goes something like this:

> When I was young, I set out to change the world. When I grew a little older, I perceived that this was too ambitious, so I set out to change my country. This, too, I realized as I grew older was too ambitious, so I set out to change my community. When I realized that I could not even do this, I tried to change my family. Now, as an old man, I know that I should have started with myself; maybe then I would have succeeded in changing my family, the community, and, who knows, maybe even the world.

There are many reasons why schools have not been transformed in the past, and why students are being left unprepared for their future careers and lives. The question is not who is to blame, the question is how do we transform education? Many teachers are already taking more control over their teaching and giving their students more control over their learning. Teachers are figuring out how to incorporate many of the ideas discussed in this chapter and in the rest of this book. These teachers have decided to just do what they know in their hearts is right for their students.

Transformation, in the view of the present authors, has to be in the hands of the people on the ground: teachers, students, and principals. Each individual teacher, principal, and school has to decide it is time for educators and students to retake control of public education in our nation.

Educators have to say, "Enough." Enough of people with political agendas telling educators how and what to teach; enough of people who want to make millions of dollars from the educational system telling educators what and how to assess; enough of allowing people who do not want to pay taxes to try to ruin public education; enough of those rich people who want to maintain their riches and power at the expense of the rest of the nation; enough of the prejudice that separates people into the haves and the have-nots, into the in-groups and the out-groups, and those who are saved and those who have to be saved from themselves.

Amanda Bastoni (chapter 4) discusses how teachers are beginning to feel the shift to more student-centered approaches. Traditional high schools and technical high schools are beginning to work together more collaboratively in the best interests of their students. Now more educators have to take advantage of this moment in time to transform education from the inside-out. In this book the authors advocate for Robinson's (2017) assumptions:

1. We are living in times of revolutionary change.
2. We have to think differently about the talents and abilities of our students and teachers.
3. We have to run schools, companies, and communities differently. (p. 5)

The present authors have operationalized those ideas and, for this book, have created the following additional four assumptions:

1. Our educational systems must be transformed.
2. That transformation should be led by educators.
3. Each student has to be valued in every school and in every classroom.
4. Success looks different for each student.

If educators seriously consider these ideas and other ideas they have read, heard, or developed through individual contemplations, the correct path will become clear. Then, remembering we are not alone, educators can decide what they want for their own children or grandchildren, and what teachers want for their students. It is time!

Chapter 2

A Call for Change From Within the Classroom

Christopher Geraghty

Coupled with the squeaking of whiteboard marker drawings that animate his points in an RSA Animate video titled, *Changing the education paradigm*, Sir Ken Robinson and the RSA (2010) weaves together a justification that the current model of education is outdated and is crushing creativity in today's students. Intrigued by Robinson's (2010) points, concerning the contemporary model of public schools being stuck in the age of the Industrial Revolution, educators found themselves nodding in agreement.

The video's animation depicts a familiar scene of a student slumped in his seat, drool slowly dripping from the corner of his mouth, as the teacher stands at a board in the front of the classroom. Knowing this image is the antithesis of what teachers want for students, educators have listened to Robinson (2010) with a focus of a better education system for all students.

Today's students have access to more information and technology than any generation before them, yet knowing how to use and access information effectively is one of their greatest challenges (Wagner & Compton, 2015; Wagner & Dintersmith, 2016). The initial reaction to any question students face is to turn to Google or Siri for the answer. With the endless amounts of information and misinformation that can be accessed with a couple of clicks on a device, students struggle to think critically about the process of evaluating and analyzing information.

Robinson (2010) challenges the assumption that the factory model of education can still produce citizens capable of adapting to the fluid economy of the future. His challenge needs to be at the center of all school reform models. Robinson's (2010) call for a change to the education paradigm took place ten years ago, and yet there have been little-to-no large-scale changes to the American model of education that would truly embody a paradigm shift emphasizing creativity, collaboration, and critical thinking.

Robinson's (2010) overall message from ten years ago focused on schools needing to break the existing model by fostering, accepting, and celebrating multiple forms of intelligence and skills as necessary elements of modern education. This call for change is even more paramount today. Robinson (2017) himself revisits this same call for transformation with his book, *Out of our minds: The power of being creative* (2017), while highlighting the snail's pace at which schools are responding to the need for change.

Schools, and those within the system of public education, need to face the reality that a diversity of talents is needed within society, and that "college and career" ready means many different things for different students. Personalization needs to mean more than providing a student options within an assigned project within a required class. Personalized learning needs to be embodied across the curricula within schools, and students need to be supported in accessing the curricula in a variety of ways.

The traditional manner of accessing a subject area needs to be challenged by the development of more interdisciplinary models that imbed competency in multiple areas through inquiry and authentic learning environments (DiMartino & Clarke, 2008). Learning can take on many forms. Isolating content areas into their own individual courses of study is not a method that engages students in the dynamic environment that they will face outside of the school setting.

For meaningful transformation to occur, everyone invested in the current model of education will face challenges regarding change (Fullan & Langworthy, 2013, 2014). The age-old argument from the community and parents who say the current model worked for them and so it should work for their children needs to be exposed as a fallacy that will perpetuate the *status quo* and be damaging to their children's future (Abeles & Rubenstein, 2016).

Politicians that inform policy need to be exposed to the realistic challenges facing schools and break from the politics that are creating division and an unwillingness to engage in meaningful policy reform that supports student growth (Ravitch, 2010; Ravitch, 2014). Accountability measures for schools on student learning cannot rely on the standardized tests of the past that support society's acceptance of regurgitating facts and formulas as an accurate measurement of learning.

Society's focus on test scores has hindered the necessary innovation needed within schools. Innovative practitioners, free from the constraints of standardization, can energize a generation of learners who are thirsty for opportunities to pursue their passions but need the support of teachers and a community of learners.

In order to improve the educational outcomes for students, which in turn, supports social justice and further developing positive citizen involvement, public education needs to change. "School" will need to look different for different individuals. The factory model that Robinson (2017) refers to will be restructured to be more fluid. Restrictions, such as grade levels, may be thrown out with the other factory model structures. Moving to a competency-based system that truly embodies the concept of skill development and knowledge acquisition will be necessary for real personalized learning to take place for all students.

There are many existing assumptions that would be challenged in creating such reform, but it can be done. It will demand political capital and investment from a multitude of the groups and individuals within communities, but the outcome will better support the entire community.

ASSUMPTIONS THAT MUST BE SHATTERED

The meaning of an innovative school has changed over time. Many schools once built with no classroom walls, as part of the open concept design movement during the 1970s, have now transformed to resemble the traditional public high school (George & Florida Educational Research and Development Council, 1975)—concrete block walls, tones that sound at the beginning and end of the periods, departments organized in different parts of the building, and students reporting to designated locations at designated times.

Innovative educators within "traditional" looking schools can be agents of change. Over time creative educators can develop the autonomy and time with students to confront traditional assumptions that are limiting the education of students. These same limiting assumptions are those that must be shattered to create the innovative educational environment that all students deserve.

Standardization

The American public school system is focused on standardized tests and accountability measures that kill creative pedagogy (Ravitch, 2010; Robinson & Aronica, 2016). Implementing and continuing the standardized measurement tools created with the No Child Left Behind legislation of George W. Bush's administration, the American public system of education is retreating from the progressive initiatives that can improve the educational experiences of students (Ravitch, 2010). There is a danger of negating the strength within the American system that is the opportunity to experience a contest mobility system (Zhao, 2009).

Zhao (2009) identifies a contest mobility system as a system that provides students the opportunity to experiment in order to find their passion for a career. For greater numbers of schools to embrace a contest mobility system that benefits students, the standardization movement must be confronted in its current state. Curriculum and instruction must be reimagined to provide all students an agreed upon baseline of common curriculum while also fostering opportunities for personalization and creativity.

When discussing how schools have either supported or hindered their learning throughout their time in public education with a group of current high school students, the author identified a common theme that school is too rigid for all. One student's comment highlights the group's opinion:

> School is too structured. Yes, there are things that we should all learn and be able to do, but too much is focused on the same experiences for everyone. They [public schools] treat us all the same and we're definitely not, and schools shouldn't be graded based upon standardized tests. Those tests don't tell you what we [students] really know, can do, or even care about. Schools need to be more about the individual students and, yes, some common skills and knowledge are important, but that should be taken care of in the early grades and by the time students reach high school there should be a lot more freedom to pursue student interests, while still learning skills to help us outside of school.

This comment illustrates the valuing of universal content and skills that all students should learn, but it also demonstrates the awareness of flaws in the standardization system that is preventing a more dynamic learning experience for all students.

Contributing to the call for the shattering of the standardization movement, the National Center for Education Statistics (2015) indicates that four-year national high school dropout rates fluctuated between 10.9 percent and 6.6 percent during the time period of 2000–2014. Additionally, the 2014 Gallup Education study reports only 55 percent of students and 33 percent of teachers feel engaged and hopeful for the educational future (Blad, 2017). According to the 2018 statistics from the National Center for Education Statistics, for 2015–2016, approximately 2.3 million students, who had not graduated, were not enrolled in any school.

Blad (2017) argues, teachers have become disengaged from their educational communities. Accountability measures focused on improving test scores, such as No Child Left Behind (U.S. Department of Education, 2002) and Race to the Top (U.S. Department of Education, 2009), have hindered a teacher's ability to create innovative educational experiences for all students. Instead of being focused on innovative practice to engage student critical thinking and collaboration, professional development has focused on tracking, reporting, and improving test scores.

Accountability based upon standardized testing is contrary to Zhao's (2009) argument presenting creative pedagogy and critical thinking as the strengths of the American education system. Being forced to implement specific lesson plans geared toward improving test scores saps the teaching professional's desire to engage in the more challenging and engaging lines of inquiry that students deserve (Borman et al., 2002).

Politicians and state leaders must break free of the restrictive and punitive measures of legislation such as No Child Left Behind (U.S. Department of Education, 2002) and Race to the Top (U.S. Department of Education, 2009), allowing school leaders and educators to develop a more dynamic and responsive feedback and progress monitoring system for their students (Fullan, Hargreaves, & Rincon-Gallardo, 2015). For such changes to occur, schools need driven leaders, engaged educators (Hargreaves & Goodson, 2006), and inspired students (Preble & Gordon, 2011).

Student Agency

Schools are created to educate students. This statement embodies the assumption that schools are a place where students go to be educated, to be recipients of the process, and harkens to Robinson and the RSA's (2010) Animate video illustrating a student's brain being filled with information from the teacher. This passive approach to learning must be changed to students being agents of their learning, actively engaging and shaping their learning experiences (Couros, 2015; Spencer & Juliani, 2016).

Agency is one's ability to impact change. Student agency is paramount in supporting student engagement with learning that is internalized and applied to later challenges one will face (Couros, 2015; Juliani, 2015; MacKenzie, 2016; Sousa, 2016, 2017). Students want to be active and involved in shaping their own learning, and increasing student agency increases engagement and excitement about learning (MacKenzie, 2016).

Current trends in education attempting to improve schools and meet the needs of twenty-first-century schools include increasing "student voice" within school culture and increasing Science, Technology, Engineering, and Mathematics (STEM) offerings within school curriculum, but these initiatives are missing the mark at what will truly transform learning in schools. It is student inquiry and student agency that are the most meaningful concepts that must be embraced to change the assumption of students being recipients of information, to students becoming excited and engaged in their learning as active inquisitive participants (Couros, 2015; Spencer & Juliani, 2016).

Student voice is a part of the process to developing student agency, and STEM is a means to employ inquiry-based learning (Couros, 2015). A secondary school educator of eighteen years that carries the title of school STEM coordinator recently stated:

> It's not STEM that we want to teach students, it's getting them engaged and being creative in their approach to problem solving. The "STEM" or "STEAM" titles for classes are current education buzz words, but it is actually holding us back in my opinion. Titles like this make teachers and students alike think that, "Now it's time to STEM and work on some creative project." No, this is not what we want, we want inquiry across the entire school. We want students to face thoughtful and challenging questions, and for them to create their own tough questions that push them to confront difficult issues that the world is facing. Having things like a Maker Space and classes that look at STEM-based projects or competitions are great, but that's not what our overall goal should be. Our goal should be to support students in the ability to ask challenging questions that require them to struggle with content and develop skills to enhance their learning in all subject areas. Ultimately this work should be interdisciplinary and I think will drive what school is going to need to look like in the future.

Inquiry-based learning requires student and teacher collaboration in creating compelling questions that demand research, collaboration, critical thinking, and authentic application of learning (Juliani, 2015; MacKenzie, 2016). Inquiry-based learning demands student agency, in that students develop the skills to voice their desire to shape their learning through an organized and at times fluid curriculum (MacKenzie, 2016).

Embracing inquiry-based learning incorporates the process of questioning, and in developing this skill, students can tackle any issues they may face in the future. Having a school with an inquiry approach requires a shift from teachers as distributors of information to teachers as coaches and guides in student learning (Wagner & Compton, 2015).

Students have a vested interest in shaping their own learning, and intrinsic motivation increases with their agency (Pink, 2012). When a system is developed to support students in developing the skills to shape their learning around their passions, schools will be adopting a model of education for the twenty-first-century student. With such a shift, schools can transform from a place where students are educated to a place where students can be supported in learning to learn, while developing skills that will help them enter an ever-changing world.

Assessment

A frustrating assumption that educators confront around assessment of student learning is that the grade a student earns on any assessment is the most important thing for a student to focus on within their education. The pressure students face in achieving high grades is at the heart of the 2010 film, *Race to Nowhere* (Abeles & Congdon, 2010), in which the daily struggle to "make the grade" and live up to the expectations associated with going to college outweigh the process and interest in learning that students previously held.

Crippled by stress and anxiety, students focus on the grade found on their transcript and the impact it will have on their future opportunities. Student learning could be much more impactful if the focus was on the process of actually learning and not the grade used to measure skill development and knowledge acquisition (Abeles & Congdon, 2010; Abeles & Rubenstein, 2016).

With a shift away from the traditional earning of credit for coursework through achieving a letter grade based upon a hundred-point scale, the implementation of competency-based education is attempting to refocus schools on developing mastery of specific competencies (Dintersmith, 2018). Coupled with this change in grading, schools have an opportunity to embrace further innovations.

New Hampshire high schools have recently transitioned to a competency-based education model with student learning being assessed on levels of proficiency within multiple competencies in each course. The catalyst for this transition came from the New Hampshire Department of Education's policy of scrapping the use of seat time-based Carnegie credits for graduation and replacing the assessment systems with competency requirements for graduation (Bramante & Colby, 2012).

With the implementation of competency-based assessment practices, there have been many philosophical and practical discussions among school faculty and community members about how to best support students' learning. This change has demanded the use of more remediation supports for students and a change in teachers' mindsets to support students in developing their skills and knowledge to reach at least a basic level of proficiency in a more personalized manner.

Earning credit in a course now requires basic proficiency being demonstrated by students in all competency areas in a particular course. This practice breaks from the traditional final grade being the result of the averages of all assessment scores or weighted categories. A student's level of learning is reported in a more detailed and comprehensive manner with skills and knowledge being delineated into multiple competencies in the course. This process provides greater accuracy in reporting of student skill development and knowledge acquisition making the grades more relevant to what students know and can do.

Fully implementing competency-based grading has also challenged teachers to reflect upon their own instructional and assessment practices. Competency-based grading demands that assessments be designed with a greater level of intent when assessing different competencies within a course. In doing so, competency-based grading blends well with authentic assessments that challenge students to connect skills and content knowledge affiliated with a particular field of study. Such authentic assessments also lend themselves to multidisciplinary collaboration that better reflects the authentic work and situations students will face after high school.

Authentic scenarios support increasing the personalization of assessment practices within the curriculum and lead to greater levels of engagement and novelty in learning (DiMartino, Wolk, & Curtis, 2010; Sousa, 2017). A New Hampshire high school educator who is a self-described traditional teacher and was initially very skeptical of competency-based grading stated:

> Competency based grading has made me reflect more about what we are doing here. I'm in the business of helping students learn to contribute to society, and if they fail a test of mine and then we just keep going, what good is that for anyone? With the competency-based system, I feel like I have permission to go back with that one student and work with them to more clearly identify what they know and can do. Whereas, in the past we'd keep moving along as a group and that one student would have to try and keep up. I also feel like the shift to competencies has reinvigorated my creativity. I now work with students to develop ways for them to demonstrate what they know instead of me creating a test to see what they know and don't know.

This educator is emphasizing the personalized nature of what implementing competency-based assessments can do, if the assessments are accompanied by a change in mindset to support student growth in an equitable manner.

However, the reality is that this New Hampshire educator still sees 110 students during their school's eight-period day. Without additional structural changes to the traditional regimented systems of schools, competency-based assessment will illustrate the need for students to remediate work to truly learn, but there would be no means to do so, thus perpetuating the *status quo*.

Scheduling

The use of time within a school can directly impact the culture and outcomes for student learning. Whether it is a version of block scheduling or a seven-period day, schools are seeking an effective use of time. A New Hampshire public high school with a well-established school culture supporting flexibility among the faculty for student schedules incorporates a creative use of time that honors student and teacher autonomy.

This school utilizes a seven-period day, no bells, and classes meeting four days per week with the fifth day being utilized at the discretion of the teacher.

Students are not scheduled into study halls during "free periods," but are instead free to visit any of the subject-specific resource areas in the building or access open campus upon entering tenth grade. This was and is not the norm of public schools across the country.

With the majority of schools in the United States employing a version of block scheduling or a five- to seven-period day, students have their time managed for them (DiMartino & Clarke, 2008; Robinson & Aronica, 2016). Working in a system that has students and school faculty trained to drop an in-depth discussion or engaging experiment due to a tone sounding the end of that period of time is a detriment to the learning experiences of students. Learning in the twenty-first century needs to embrace the multidisciplinary mantra being presented by innovative schools across the nation that are breaking from the traditional scheduling of student time into segregated content areas that prevent collaboration across disciplines (Dintersmith, 2018).

Many schools across New Hampshire have adopted the use of a flexible scheduling block during the day to support student remediation and enrichment opportunities associated with competency-based grading practices. With the development of simple-to-use software, schools are able to create and modify student learning sessions while tracking attendance of all students in the building.

This technology paired with calls for more personalized blocks of time for students to engage in a student-driven or cocurricular learning (DiMartino et al., 2010) presents schools with an opportunity for change. Schools can now have the tools and justification to blow up the traditional factory model dependent upon the scheduling of a students' time as a necessity to structure student learning.

With the right planning, leadership, and processes in place it would benefit all students for schools to embrace the use of flexible scheduling software to create completely personalized schedules for all students and faculty. It is possible to have educators available for tutorials, planned lessons, work sessions, enrichment opportunities, and co-taught courses all in one day or throughout a week's time.

Such a system would transform the use of time during the school day, not only for students but also for all individuals within the existing system. This would truly transform the school day in the manner referenced by Robinson and the RSA (2010) in his *Changing the educational paradigm* talk from ten years ago. Such a change demands the previously discussed traditional assumptions regarding standardization, student agency, and assessment to also be confronted to ensure that every student is valued with a personalized use of their time.

VALUING EVERY STUDENT

Attending what is considered a top-tier high school in a state does not guarantee that students feel valued or experience a challenging and meaningful education. Often, students who attend top-ranked high schools express that they feel as if the system has treated them as another batch that has been produced by the system. Teachers being experts in their content areas, and an expectation of students mastering large amounts of information, does not equate to a quality education for individual students.

Students who can retain and then regurgitate memorized information on traditional assessments succeed in such systems. If the true goal of social studies education is creating citizens that can think critically about their surrounding world, then teachers must directly challenge existing accepted practices. A practice employed by an "exemplary teacher" at a top-notch New England high school illustrates the system churning out test takers instead of thinkers.

In this teacher's honors U.S. History course, assessments consisted of multiple choice questions. Students were provided the questions and multiple choice answers ahead of time as a means to prepare for the tests. The intent was to help students learn the content for the assessment, but instead of delving deeply into the issues of U.S. History, students simply memorized the correct answer for each question.

This practice became so ingrained in these students that to save precious time, they focused on memorizing the wording of correct answers without even reading the questions. The focus was on the grade, not learning. There is no critical thought or problem-solving associated with such an assessment, and therefore it is superficial to engage in the process.

Learning in such a rote and standardized manner disenfranchises students. Feeling valued as an individual in a school can drastically alter the educational experiences of students. Impactful teachers, who are remembered by their students, connect life experiences and challenges to the learning process. A personal connection between one's life and the content they are attempting to master will lead to long-term retention and understanding (Sousa, 2017).

Applying one's own interests within a broader content area or allowing personalized proposals for one's own method of demonstrating learning are steps to personalizing education. These are the moments, and the teachers, that inspire curiosity and can foster a passion for learning and education. The teachers who spend the time to get to know students and personalize education are the teachers who support critical thinking and inquiry.

Developing such skills prepare individuals for postsecondary educational experiences and the workforce. Public education needs to value each student in order to engage in the essential process of preparing students to enter society as individuals who can learn and adapt to an ever-changing society.

Family and Socioeconomic Influence

Public schools are the most important institution in a democratic society that seeks to embrace equity and social justice. In *Our kids: The American dream in crisis*, Robert D. Putnam (2016) highlights the significance of education as a means for social and economic advancement. Yet, in the United States, impoverished communities lack the ability to properly fund and afford the youth of such communities a stable learning environment that can provide the opportunity for economic growth.

Despite some students having equitable access to quality schools, familial levels of education are some of the strongest indicators of the future "success" of children. Parent levels of education can predict their engagement and economic ability to support and advocate for their children within school that then correlate to future economic stability and growth (Putnam, 2016). Parents with lower levels of education face economic instability and are less able to be engaged with their child's education, thus negatively impacting their child's ability to break free from their levels of poor education and poverty (Putnam, 2016).

Cultural Impact on Learning

Such factors as the previously stated economic inequities in school funding and the impact of families upon student learning are outside of the control of schools. There are factors that impact the valuing of students as individuals that are within the control of educators. Many of the most impactful elements upon a student's ability to learn in school can be addressed by a positive and supportive school climate that can be shaped by the actions of and relationships created by educators with their students (Hammond, 2015).

Cultural awareness and educators becoming more cognizant of their own cultural assumptions and implicit bias will assist educators in the process of establishing learning partnerships that allow learning to take place. Hammond's (2015) research on culturally responsive teaching and Sousa's research on brain (2016, 2017) support the argument that students are biologically unable to learn if they are feeling threatened or unwelcomed in a learning environment.

Many educators do not fully appreciate the lasting negative impact that unintended negative cultural comments or actions can have on a student's ability to learn. The key point here is that it is not often a choice on the student's behalf when they appear to be retracting from their involvement with their learning, but it can be due to some past trauma and microaggressions that are triggering a biological response to protect oneself (Hammond, 2015).

For these reasons, it is imperative that educators practice culturally responsive teaching that is in tune with students in the learning environment. Such practices enhance the learning experiences of all students, increase student engagement, and facilitate students transitioning from dependent to independent learners (Hammond, 2015).

Students' Perspectives

As a part of the *Inquiry and STEAM Ed.* course collaboratively developed with students and teachers, the design team in the author's school surveyed students about their experiences in the system of public education. The goal of this process was to improve the learning experiences of students in the school.

Through the process of collaborative action research, students, educators, and administrators developed new school programming that is inquiry-based, student-centered, interdisciplinary, and focused on authentic assessments. This process resulted in students taking informed action in their community. Such a course would not have been developed without the voices of students being part of the collaborative process.

When asked about their experiences in public school, students had a variety of responses with the overall trend of beginning with negative statements, followed by the positive aspects of their educational experiences. One student stated, "I feel as though school is too structured, kids in high school should be able to go down the paths that they want to, instead of having the same requirements as everyone else." This statement illustrates a common theme of students feeling restricted and therefore less willing to engage with the learning process.

A second student responded:

> Public education is a perfect example of why tradition and the tendency to resist change is limiting. It is hard to become inspired by an outdated system in which, in my opinion, it destroys the important aspects that make us human and allow us more creative and free flowing minds.

This student is essentially agreeing with Robinson's (2017) discussion about schools killing the creativity of their students and trying to push them all through the same industrial model of education.

Students are incredibly insightful about their own desires and motivation to learn, and when they can have agency in the process of learning, they will be able to assist educators in meeting their own needs. This, however, is only possible when students are comfortable with their teachers and when students' ideas and voices are honored as valid (Hammond, 2015).

To clarify, the previous statement is not advocating that all students be given free rein over their own education. Teachers do need to honor the student's perspective to develop a working relationship with each student to ensure that they are valued and provided the supports and opportunities necessary for learning.

In seeking further feedback from students in the *Inquiry and STEAM Ed.* course referenced earlier, students completed a questionnaire about whether they feel that their school and teachers are valuing them as individuals. Their responses established two significant trends that research (Hammond, 2015) also supports for students in other situations: (1) students feel valued when teachers provide individualized instruction and (2) students feel valued when teachers take the time to get to know their students by working with them as partners and by embracing student agency.

One student's response illustrates their experience as a student that feels valued based upon their interactions with their teachers:

> I think that many of my teachers show that they value you when they are willing to go out of their way to find a tool to help you. I think another way is when they go out of their way to check in on you, stay after with you, grade that one paper quickly, and at the end of the day ask you how everything is going, how your life is in and out of school is going. When they ask how your game went yesterday or know if you won or lost in the championships. I think you can tell when a teacher cares, if they care about you on a school level, but also hope that you are succeeding in other areas. In the past I've had teachers show they care when they talk about their options about the school or things going on, because we know that not everything is perfect, and to know that you are looking out and trying to make this experience as amazing as possible.

Accomplishing what this student describes takes effort and organization on the part of the educators in schools.

Establishing strong learning relationships as described by this student requires teachers to embrace student voice and the process of personalizing the educational experiences for students. Such practices return to the previously discussed assumptions around standardization, student agency, assessment, and scheduling that must be shattered. In doing so, schools can further build a culture that acknowledges and values success looking different for each individual student.

PERSONALIZED SUCCESS

Educators are quick to recognize that every student is a unique individual that comes to them with their own experiences. Yet many schools continue to perpetuate the use of standardized assessments and graduation requirements for all students. The baseline of graduation requirements is most often established at the state level, and at times local school boards create additional requirements.

Although there is a foundation of knowledge and skills that all students should master within their education, schools need to develop more flexible programming and paths to graduation. Personalizing the high school experience to each student seems like a daunting task. This seems challenging mainly because people attempt to envision personalizing within the existing industrial model of schools. As Robinson (2017) discusses, schools do not need to reform, they need to transform.

Horn (2002) explains educational reform as a process of improving a school's deficiencies without drastically altering the system or design. Educational change requires public involvement due to transformations taking place to the structural design of the system. Change and transformation are what are required to personalize the public school systems for all students. For schools to truly personalize, they will need to embrace the use of technology, develop an inquiry-based learning culture, and establish flexible uses of time.

Technology Supports Differentiation and Personalization

Technology provides educators the tools to personalize all aspects of the educational experience. With tools such as Google Classroom and other online software that can create seamless integration of videos, online assessments, and access the endless databases, educators need to embrace the opportunities before them.

Juliani (2015) highlights the use of technology as a means for educators to support student-developed inquiries leading to increased student engagement and higher levels of critical thinking. Technology can serve to assist in the daunting task of educators managing the workflow of multiple students who are working on individualized instruction and assessments.

Technology is not the answer to all learning for students, as there is an increasing need for face-to-face peer interactions and collaboration. However, technology must be embraced by educators as resource that can support truly personalized and transformed school experiences.

Inquiry at Work in the Classroom

Inquiry-based learning that is student-centered, similar to the work of Juliani (2015) and MacKenzie (2016), is challenging the existing educational paradigm of the traditional classroom. The author's school recently implemented a new course that is completely inquiry-based with students engaging in their own inquiries that they have co-constructed with the assistance of their teacher.

This *Inquiry and STEAM Ed.* course empowers students to develop compelling questions, complete research, and communicate their findings in a manner that the students design. Students have developed inquiries addressing the following compelling questions:

- In what ways has literature impacted the public's perception of war?
- How can one create the most efficient Minecraft world?
- To what extent are the scientific theories presented in the film *Interstellar* a true reflection of fact?
- In what ways has the evolution of women's basketball from the 1800s been a representation of society's evolution?
- What are the best strategies to travel in the most cost-efficient manner?
- How has the genre of short fiction literature evolved over time?
- In what ways can students positively impact their community through service trips and service learning?

With each of these student-generated compelling questions, the students identify the standards and competencies they address through their inquiry. The teacher of this class fulfills the role of advisor and guide.

Without the use of technology as a means to share work between teacher and student, the management of supporting and assessing multiple, very different inquiries could become cumbersome and therefore hold back students in their pursuit of their interests. However, with the ability to collaborate digitally, a teacher is able to support students in a timely manner and access their work to monitor progress and provide suggestions.

Pairing this online support and weekly check-in meetings with students during a scheduled daily class period creates an engaging educational environment. One student described his experience in the class as follows:

> This class has made me see everything I was missing while I was just in the regular classes. Now that I am in this class, I now know the strict path I was set on in the regular classes. I have selected topics of study in this class that I truly have a passion for; science and math related to film and things in society that I find interesting. I want to pursue a career in science and math, but this class has allowed me to explore areas of this content that I wouldn't have been able to in other classes.

A second student elaborated upon their experiences in school and discusses how the freedom and personalized nature of the *Inquiry and STEAM Ed.* course has supported their ability to learn:

> This class is unlike any other class I've ever taken. It allows students to explore education that they have never been allowed to explore before. It has allowed us

students to explore our own thoughts and wonders. It's a great opportunity for students to see how self-motivated they really are as an individual, and also push yourself to question things that you never have before. I think this learning style should be incorporated into more classes starting at younger ages, and I think every student should have the opportunity to take a course like this.

Advocating for the freedom to develop their own lines of inquiry in other classes is certainly possible, and leveraging the available technology systems and software by schools could make this happen.

The pedagogical shift from teacher-led instruction to a student-centered approach associated with greater levels of personalization and inquiry must also take place. Another student enrolled in the *Inquiry and STEAM Ed.* course stated:

This class opens the door to a whole world of possibilities that just regular classes don't. The teacher only steps in when necessary, which allows the students to struggle on a topic, which in-turn allows them to learn, and learn their way. The teacher is aware of everything that we are studying and will assist us, but only after we have struggled to find a path to answering our questions. The teacher challenges us with follow up questions and possible suggestions to get started in addressing our questions, but the teacher does not tell us what we have to do. This gives us all a sense of ownership and responsibility over our own learning.

Comments such as these from students make teachers wish to teach like this all day long, yet there is a hesitation to make transformative changes for all students. Juliani (2015) views public school systems perpetuating the *status quo* instead of embracing the transformation advocated for by Robinson (2010) and instead seeks to create change in his own classes.

Teachers could close their classroom door at the beginning of each class period in the day and create a transformation to the teaching and learning within their classroom. For systematic change to occur, it is necessary that these transformations to learning take place school-wide and the school day can no longer emulate the factory floor model of regimented schedules for all. With the support and permission of school leadership, teachers have created a glimpse of what schools need to embrace with the *Inquiry and STEAM Ed.* course model. Yet schools with such courses are still operating within the industrial model that is constraining the ability to truly transform learning.

Adaptive Scheduling

The standard school day must change and schools do have the resources to make this happen. It is whether the school can harness the technology, develop a clear vision for a flexible learning environment, and create a culture of learning that embodies personalization and authenticity in assessment that will determine the success of a transformed school with an adaptive scheduling model.

The issue of school safety and knowing where students are within the school environment are certainly important issues to consider when looking at school transformations with a flexible schedule. With new technology, there are now tools and processes that can be put in place to assist with these structural elements that impact learning.

Adaptive scheduling software exists that allows schools to develop their own blocks of time; assign teachers to these time periods; and enable students, teachers, or administrators to schedule or "book" students into these blocks of time. Such technology is now widely being used in schools across New Hampshire that have implemented a flexible time block for student remediation and enrichment.

Schools are using such software for students during enrichment/remediation blocks. Teachers are creating their own offerings, and students are booking themselves to be with the teachers they need to see or for the enrichment opportunities they would like to attend. Attendance is taken through these systems and a student's whereabouts is known.

Seeing the effective use of this technology demonstrates that the door has been thrown open to establish a system in which the entire school day could be developed on such a flexible model of time. With proper planning and an embrace of competency-based education that implements an inquiry-based learning model, schools can develop a school day that promotes student agency in learning and a collaborative environment.

Students may be working for prolonged periods of time on one inquiry in one classroom with one teacher for the majority of one day. The next day, that same student could be scheduled to attend a mathematics lesson for part of the day, a Socratic seminar for another part of the day, and then work on a collaborative project for the remainder of the day. Challenging all parties in the educational field to think differently about the use of time is an essential piece to creating an educational transformation.

In *What school could be: Insights and inspiration from teachers across America*, Dintersmith (2018) describes schools across the United States that are whittling away at the traditional assumptions that have been restricting school transformation. Regarding the use of time, Dintersmith includes a discussion of Sanborn School District, which is a member of New Hampshire's PACE (Performance Assessment of Competency Education) schools:

> They've shifted to an entirely student-centered environment for all schools—elementary, middle, and high school. Students design their own schedules, often

working in a classroom for hours at a time immersed in projects. Many courses are integrated across traditional subject boundaries. Even traditional classes look different—no students sitting passively in rows listening to a lecture. To move to the next level, students must demonstrate in–depth mastery of the material. (pp. 187–88)

The use of time needs to be thought of differently, and the traditional restraints of school schedules need to be broken down to develop a dynamic flexible learning environment. Dintersmith (2018) includes his discussion of Sanborn School District to emphasize the importance of leaders embracing opportunities to affect change on elements within the school system that can lead to broader changes to the educational experiences of all students.

CHANGE FROM THE INSIDE OUT

"Be the change you wish to see in the world," is a quote attributed to Mahatma Gandhi and is a concept that educators must embrace to effect real transformation in schools. At the end of Dintersmith's (2018) book, *What school could be: Insights and inspiration from teachers across America*, he includes a fictitious yet inspirational speech of a politician laying out a plan for transformational and cohesive educational policy. However, this speech is followed by the following:

> Don't hold your breath. We're not likely to hear this from a politician soon, maybe ever. State and national policies may never make much sense. We'll only be exasperated if we expect real change to come from our putative leaders. But here's the deal. Schools won't change from the top. They'll change on classroom, one school, one district at a time. And local change is achievable change. . . . People are connecting the dots. They're starting to see that we need to do better things in our schools, for our children. They're sensing the unbounded possibilities if we turn our students loose on problems they care about. They're ready to trust our teachers to engage and inspire our students. And as I learned so emphatically on this trip, once someone sees what school could be, there's no turning back. (pp. 219–20)

This concluding paragraph to a book that is full of examples of educators taking action to transform schools embodies Margaret Meade's quote, "Never doubt that a small group of thoughtful committed citizens can change the world. Indeed, it is the only thing that ever has." This quote has been proven true time after time in history, and research tells us that this is the case for schools as well. Educators need to take action to change their schools from the inside out if they truly care about meeting the needs of all of their students.

Research Supports Internally Driven Change

Elmore (2007) argues that educators are best positioned to influence educational reform; however, educators are underutilized as effective agents of change. Instead, teachers are the recipients of change initiatives, or they are implementers of externally provided reform efforts.

Enabling educators to act as agents of change can increase investment in the school community and ultimately support the development of a school culture that invests in innovative practices. As Hargreaves and Fullan (2012) discuss, the development of the professional capital among educators necessary to effectively achieve internally driven change can be questioned in many schools unless there are intentional structural and cultural steps taken to support such efforts.

Additionally, students need to have meaningful voice in the development of school programming in order to establish an invested and relevant role within the school community (Diera, 2016). Such an investment in school culture can improve student relationships with peers as well as the adults in their school community (Preble & Gordon, 2011) and ultimately support the development of a school culture that invests in innovative practices (DiMartino & Clarke, 2008)

Collaborative Action Research

Without the active involvement of educators and students as change agents, initiatives for change may face increased resistance and are likely to receive less support from the educators best situated to impact the fidelity of the initiative (Elmore, 2007). To transform schools, those within the schools will need to take the lead. As Dintersmith (2018) argues, real change will take place at the local level.

To achieve such change educators and students should partner and undertake collaborative action research that can lead to new school programming that can collectively demand structural transformations of schools. The well-established steps of collaborative action research include the process of (1) identifying a focus, (2) collecting data, (3) analyzing and interpreting the data, (4) acting based upon the data, (5) reflection, followed by (6) continued modifications to the focus area (Gall, Gall, & Borg, 2007; Sagor, 1992, 2000, 2005). For collaborative action research to result in impactful change, there must be the support of school leadership and engagement by those in the school (Sagor, 1992).

CONCLUSIONS

Participating in collaborative action research can result in real changes to school programming. The development process of the *Inquiry and STEAM Ed.*

course previously referenced in this chapter was created due to a group of dedicated educators and students engaging in collaborative action research. The process began with the group holding focus groups with students to seek input about what could be improved in the school.

There was no focus other than improving the experiences of students. After the change team analyzed the input of students and faculty, a proposal of the *Inquiry and STEAM Ed.* course was developed and shared for feedback. Following multiple drafts of the course proposal and continuous feedback from students, faculty, and administration, the new course was added as an offering at our school.

The process of creating this new class and the different approach to learning that it provides compared to the school's other classes has sparked greater calls for change within the school. With these calls for change comes a necessary process of self-reflection as a school about what is best for students.

Difficult discussions are forcing those in the community to challenge traditional assumptions about what school is, and what school could be and needs to be in the future. Knowing that change needs to occur, there is a call for action to take place at the local level, and with momentum over time these local changes can drive state-level change.

Robinson's (2010) and Robinson and Aronica's (2016) call for an overhaul and transformation is inspiring, yet Dintersmith's (2018) points regarding change taking place at the local level leading to greater change across the field of public education is the practical approach that can lead to an eventual transformation. Educators, students, administrators, and community members who are directly involved with their community's schools are those who will create the necessary changes for the future. These individuals must become the whistleblowers that collaborate to transform our schools into the dynamic learning environments that all students deserve.

Chapter 3

Eliminating Exams From Gateway College Mathematics Courses: Going beyond Corequisite Mathematics

Richard A. Andrusiak

The corequisite reform movement is one of the recent efforts to restructure and improve entry-level college curricula. The creation of corequisite mathematical sequences for entry-level college mathematics courses has gained considerable momentum in the past few years, largely due to the efforts of Complete College America (CCA). These entry-level courses are often referred to as gateway courses. These courses serve as the entry points into program and major courses, or more likely, the exit points for the majority of students.

Corequisite models are a direct response to the repeated well-documented failure of developmental mathematics programs intended to remediate underprepared students. Only 30 percent of students pass all of the developmental mathematics courses in which they enroll (Attewell et al., 2006). The situation appears bleaker when you consider that, nationally, only 20 percent of students who begin in developmental mathematics courses go on to complete their gateway mathematics courses within two years (Complete College America, 2016b).

Corequisite models have many different designs. Most designs are constructed to give students real-time help in their college-level mathematics courses, while addressing the gaps in skills and concepts, along with misconceptions that students hold with the underlying fundamental mathematical ideas essential for their success. Additionally, corequisite designs seek to reduce or eliminate the number of developmental courses students are required to complete.

Corequisite mathematics pathways are novel and innovative approaches that are difficult for a large portion of the mathematical community to initially accept. Many mathematics professors wonder how students can be successful in gateway courses if they lack the underlying skills for that success.

Furthermore, there is not currently a body of randomized controlled experimental designs supporting the success of corequisite models. However, while the model may be initially difficult to accept, it is built on the premise that the current situation is so dismal that any disruptive changes to developmental preparation are likely to result in better outcomes.

As Logue (2018) notes, we can still use much more research on what specific aspects of corequisite models contribute to student success; however, that is not a cause to favor a model that is less effective (i.e., the current developmental structure at most colleges). Initial positive results are being replicated across the nation and across both small and large institutions, rural and urban. And, while it may be too soon to jump to any causal relationships, the initial results are promising.

Evidence suggests that corequisite remediation is more effective than traditional models. Corequisite mathematics fits within a broader frame of two fundamental questions important to the future of education:

- How do educational and other organizations have to change to meet the challenges of our rapidly changing world?
- What do educators and other leaders say about the future of educational design in our nation and the world?

This chapter expands on how education can be transformed from within the system, by proposing how to go beyond the creation of corequisite mathematics courses. Built upon the core assumptions that education must be transformed, every student has to be valued, success looks different for each student, and transformation must begin from within the system, the purpose of this chapter is to propose eliminating exams from gateway mathematics courses. This is a first step in transforming assessment in the mathematics classroom.

The creation of corequisite mathematics sequences has resulted in increased percentages of students who are successful in gateway mathematics courses. However, increased completion percentages alone are not sufficient to ensure that students develop the critical-thinking and problem-solving skills required to be successful in a rapidly changing global society. This chapter explores:

1. core assumptions influencing the educational transformations recommended in this chapter;
2. gateway mathematics curricula reform efforts;
3. corequisite mathematics, the evaluation of corequisite mathematics, and a corequisite mathematics case study; and
4. assessment transformation, students' attitudes toward mathematics, and the call for eliminating exams from gateway mathematics courses.

CORE ASSUMPTIONS

Defining the purpose of education is often seen strictly as an academic exercise. However, it is difficult to imagine companies not regularly revisiting their missions, values, and goals if they want to remain current and viable. In a similar fashion, educational institutions should regularly review their core assumptions.

The purpose of education is a fundamental element in defining both change and reform. Change requires both public understanding and education, whereas reform requires no major investment from the public other than their agreement (Horn, 2002). The former leaves the system transformed in a significant way from its previous design, and the latter attempts to correct deficiencies within the system without changing the essential components of the system. The purpose of education is influenced by two broad perspectives: (1) a conservative perspective and (2) a liberal perspective.

Two Educational Perspectives

A conservative perspective on the purpose of education focuses on a market-oriented culture attempting to spread and preserve the dominant culture to all individuals (Horn, 2002). This perspective is often aligned with a market-based approach that emphasizes meeting the needs of business and industry. This viewpoint focuses on education as a market with educators and students as consumers. Educational reform focuses on correcting deviations from this mission swinging back toward dominant culture.

A liberal perspective aims to create informed and active citizens. This aligns to a philosophical perspective of education seeking to preserve democratic ideals. Reform focuses on correcting any deviations from this mission and supports the ideal of transformation of self and society (Horn, 2002). In this model, people believe that education should help students think critically and develop character to function as productive citizens in a democratic society.

Regardless of which perspective you support (or come closest to supporting), it is difficult to deny that schools are still based upon late nineteenth- and early twentieth-century standards to train farmers and shopkeepers to be factory workers and office managers (Davidson, 2017). The factory model of schools hinders customized learning for students and obstructs the creation of student-centric schools (Christensen, Horn, & Johnson, 2011).

The influence of the factory model of education can be witnessed in the majority of K-12 schools across America.

- Bells ring to signal the end of classes.
- Students move from class to class on strict schedules with little academic freedom.

- Existing content area silos create little opportunity for collaboration throughout the academic day.
- Each teacher does their own part to move students through an assembly line of offerings.

Colleges are losing their relevancy in helping students succeed in a complex world. They continue to ignore neuroscience research which supports that we all learn differently and at different rates. In 2001, Steen noted that the current mathematics curriculum is built off nineteenth-century European mathematics that spread across the world during colonialism. Too little has changed since 2001 as too many high schools continue to promote the calculus track as the dominant pathway at the expense of quantitative literacy and statistical reasoning. And, we continue to believe that our schools are failing based upon an obsession with test taking.

The School Failure Fallacy

The school failure fallacy is largely based upon valuing a nation of test takers. Moreover, there is a pervasive view that students in the United States do not perform particularly well on international assessments, especially in science and mathematics. Ravitch (2014) debunks this viewpoint calling it unfounded as scores on the National Assessment of Educational Progress are at all-time highs for students who are white, black, Hispanic, and Asian and show dramatic increases in mathematics over the past two decades.

Ravitch (2014) and Zhao (2009) point to American productivity despite low test scores on international comparisons. Zhao (2009) cites the creation of core innovations during the digital revolution as a major contributing factor to the U.S. Global Competitiveness Index (GCI) rating (number 1 out of 131 countries on the 2007–2008 GCI). The United States continues to rank high on the GCI achieving a third-place ranking in the 2016–2017 report (World Economic Forum, 2016).

To some degree there is evidence that current educational assumptions are working when measured by the historical performance of the economy in the United States. However, changes in the American educational system have largely focused on our poor standing on international assessments. Standards are important to define what we value and believe all students should know and be able to do. However, devaluing some content areas in favor of others and preparing all students to know exactly the same standards devalues what is fundamentally American and results in student disengagement, teacher turnover, and low morale among both students and teachers.

In 2012, the MetLife Survey of the American Teacher found that nearly one-third of all teachers were thinking about quitting, and the Scholastic-Gates survey reported that teachers did not like the direction of current school reform (as cited in Ravitch, 2014). It is also worth noting that out of 2.1 million students tested on the ACT, only 1,258 students had an expressed and measured interest in teaching mathematics or science (ACT, 2016).

The real challenges of socioeconomic inequalities, outdated curricula, and lack of qualified teachers are not being addressed by high-stakes assessment. High-stakes testing and accountability are threats to the strengths of the American educational system, including the value of the individual, diverse talents, inclusion, and tolerance. These values lead to innovation, preparing individuals for societal changes and, ultimately, global competitiveness.

The changes in the American educational system are emulating some of our Asian counterparts who lead the way in international testing. At the same time, those countries are attempting to emulate our strengths since they know all too well the damages resulting from a high-stakes assessment-driven accountability system (Zhao, 2009). The high-stakes assessment focus of the past two decades has further driven the reliance on exams in the classroom as the primary way of measuring student performance while consuming valuable instructional time.

The assessment craze of the first part of the twenty-first century has created school failure. Many economists believe that families and families' incomes have a much greater impact on test scores than schools or teachers, estimating that as much as 60 percent of the variation in test scores is attributed to families in comparison to 20 percent to 25 percent of the variation being accounted for by schools and teachers (Ravitch, 2014). Ravitch (2014) notes that there is a lack of substantial evidence that the mandates of large-scale annual assessments have led to sustained education improvements.

The growing costs of failure are well documented. Annually, remedial courses cost students and their families about $1.3 billion across the United States and the District of Columbia (Jimenez et al., 2016). Furthermore, students who enter remedial courses are less likely to graduate (Complete College America, 2016b; Cullinane & Treisman, 2010; Jimenez et al., 2016). Ultimately, these failures create a myriad of issues, such as

- loss of monies contributed to our social security system;
- innovative and creative companies having difficulty finding the talented workforce they need to succeed;
- our growing and failing correctional system;
- the widening of the gap between the rich and the poor;
- gentrification;

- the demoralization of teachers and students within the current educational system;
- the lack of funding for public education; and
- the well-documented lack of individuals who want to seek future professions in education.

Education Needs to Be Transformed, Not Reformed

The scale and pace of technological advances and changes in society paints the picture of an exponentially increasing model, with the linear function that represents the pace of educational change well below and behind. At the heart of our educational system remains the mindset that Robinson (2017) describes as industrialism and academicism. The "system" sorts some students for the workforce and others for academics and does not necessarily recognize a connection between these facets. The needs of the workforce are rapidly changing. The advanced manufacturing of today looks scarcely like that of the Industrial Revolution.

A major assumption educators maintain is that intelligence is a function of academic intelligence. Furthermore, academic intelligence is often measured by discipline—hard versus soft sciences and Science, Technology, Engineering, and Mathematics (STEM) fields versus Humanities, English, World Languages, and Liberal Arts. It is clear by our large-scale assessment mandates and federal funding that we value some disciplines more than others. Unfortunately, students ultimately absorb this mindset.

Robinson (2017) believes that this academic illusion accounts for many of our beliefs as a society. For example, many would assume that an astrophysicist is more intelligent than everyone else in the room. The first step in transforming education is revising our vision of intelligence. Of course, this idea is not new. One only needs to look to Gardner's (1983) work with multiple intelligences.

Educators need to recognize that all individuals have unique talents and use diversity to our advantage to innovate and create (Robinson, 2017). We need to stop believing that all students need to learn and master the exact same material in the exact same time frame (e.g., common core standards). It is time to give students the opportunity to discover their talents and passions and use them to solve novel problems.

Education should focus on designing flexible learning pathways that value individualism, diversity, and inclusion and redefine what it means to teach and support learning. Educators need to think intentionally about what good assessment looks like and how to use assessment to inform learning. Student choice and autonomy and appropriate use of technology can improve student engagement (Sousa, 2016).

Instructors should promote inquiry-based learning that allows for flexible projects through competency-based assessments. Wagner (2016) describes the innovation era as happening at the boundaries of academic disciplines and organized around big ideas, questions, and problems that need solving. Schools ought to build partnerships between educational institutions, businesses and industries, and the community to create authentic learning opportunities.

Schools need to spark students' curiosities and passions while allowing them to be the architects of their own learning by taking risks and solving problems collaboratively through trial and error and iteration (Wagner, 2016). It is time to abandon the sole idea of seat time. And while educational institutions are slow to respond to change, ultimately, the economic tide is coming for them. Transformations will be necessary to stay relevant and maintain value.

There is a loss of faith in paper credentials as the skills often obtained in the academic environment do not correlate to the ability to innovate (Wagner, 2016). Educators need to rethink the curriculum and be more flexible about designing academics around habits of the mind, critical thinking, problem-solving skills, and innovation and creativity, rather than the other way around. To accomplish all this, teachers and administrators need to keep students and learning at the center of what they do. "The goal of higher education is greater than workforce readiness. It's *world* readiness" (Davidson, 2017, p. 15).

Educators need to adopt the following core assumptions that will result in fostering students' intellectual curiosities, resulting in exploring novel situations and developing creative solutions to complex problems:

- Education should not only facilitate achieving one's life goals but also facilitate thinking critically and developing character to function in society (King Jr., 1947).
- All individuals possess talent, and education should help individuals realize and develop those talents (Robinson, 2017).
- Education must value individualism, creativity, innovation, and a diversity of ideas.
- Education should be inquiry-based through collaborative opportunities with academic institutions, the community, and the workforce.
- Individuals learn at different paces and in different ways.
- Education is the gateway to closing widening inequality gaps.
- Education should focus on cultural awareness, critical-thinking skills, problem-solving skills, and habits of the mind. These should be central to the exploration of all content areas and those explorations should be built around these ideas (not the other way around).
- Education has economic, cultural, and personal goals (Robinson, 2017).

- Education should focus on social justice, equality, and service learning.
- An essential purpose of education is to develop independent learners and thinkers.

This new education is a new epistemology—one that empowers students to better their lives and thrive in a complicated world (Davidson, 2017). Many of these core assumptions align with recent gateway curricula reform efforts. Corequisite models are increasing the number of students who are successful in gateway mathematics courses based mostly on traditional assessment practices. Since those practices (i.e., tests) do not empower students, or guarantee that students develop the skills we desire, we need to merge gateway curricula reform with reevaluating how we assess student learning.

GATEWAY CURRICULA REFORM EFFORTS

This section briefly outlines some of the various mathematical curricula reforms that have surfaced in the first part of the twenty-first century that have fidelity with our core assumptions. Unfortunately, as we enter the third decade of the twenty-first century, we are still talking about making essential changes that should have happened years ago. The time is now, and transformations must begin with educators making changes within their classrooms.

As Davidson (2017) notes, too many academics are traditionalists hanging onto academic traditions, curricula, structure, and assessment methods that were developed between 1860 and 1925. These methods are no longer sufficient for preparing our graduates to deal with a rapidly changing global society. Quantitative and statistical literacy are still undervalued in a traditional curriculum, despite their importance in a changing global society.

Quantitative Literacy

The call for a focus on quantitative literacy in the curriculum gained momentum in the early part of the twenty-first century with the National Council on Education and the Disciplines release of *Mathematics and democracy: The case for quantitative literacy* (see Steen, 2001). For a historical development, see *New Hampshire PreK–16 numeracy action plan for the 21st century* (New Hampshire Department of Education, 2010). Paulos's (1988) book, *Innumeracy: Mathematical illiteracy and its consequences*, documents the individual and societal costs of having an innumerate population and is credited with bringing the issue of quantitative literacy to the mainstream public.

Quantitative literacy is difficult to define. However, what is clear is that it is different from mathematics but interacts intimately with mathematical reasoning, problem-solving, critical-thinking skills, and habits of the mind. Often, quantitative literacy involves what would appear to be simple mathematics (e.g., arithmetic) in sophisticated ways to solve novel and complex problems (New Hampshire Department of Education, 2010).

Steen (2001) lays out the elements of a comprehensive portrait of quantitative literacy that include (1) confidence with mathematics; (2) cultural appreciation; (3) interpreting data; (4) logical thinking; (5) making decisions; (6) working with mathematics in context; and (7) developing number sense, practical skills, prerequisite knowledge, and symbol sense.

Steen (2004) makes a number of salient points regarding quantitative literacy that are worth noting:

- College educators tend to believe that quantitative literacy should be developed in K-12 education rather than higher education.
- While it seems logical to house quantitative literacy efforts within a mathematical science department, we need to be careful to develop an integrated cross-disciplinary approach to quantitative literacy that allows students to analyze contexts in diverse disciplines.
- Quantitative literacy is mostly absent from accountability and assessment.
- Parents push for a calculus-driven curriculum even though research shows that it is largely ineffective in developing numeracy.
- Connections between subjects like statistics and quantitative literacy are likely stronger than those between traditional pathways such as college algebra and quantitative literacy.

Initial Twenty-First-Century Mathematical Reforms

In 1995, the American Mathematical Association of Two-Year Colleges (AMATYC) published a standards document called *Crossroads in mathematics: Standards for introductory college mathematics*, and later, followed the document in 2006 with a publication called *Beyond crossroads: Implementing mathematics standards in the first two years of college*. These documents outline curricula reform for gateway mathematics courses and integrate elements of quantitative literacy while embracing a call for continuous improvement.

In 2011, the Mathematical Association of America (MAA) released *Partner discipline recommendations for introductory college mathematics and the implications for college algebra*. The Curriculum Renewal across the First Two Years of College (CRAFTY) subcommittee of the MAA created a set of college algebra guidelines emphasizing the use of algebra and functions for modeling. These guidelines provide a foundation for the development of quantitative literacy, while addressing real-world mathematical models.

The CRAFTY document (Ganter & Haver, 2011) is an important document aimed at rethinking college algebra. Despite traditional college algebra courses largely being failures for developing quantitative literacy skills, they remain very popular choices for gateway courses (New Hampshire Department of Education, 2010). While algebra is the gateway to higher-level mathematics, as Cathy N. Davidson, professor and founder of the Futures Initiative at the Graduate Center of the City University of New York, notes in Strauss's (2017) blog, it is the single most failed course in high schools and community colleges.

This recognition has resulted in an effort to align mathematical pathways with academic focus areas (AFAs) or meta-majors. For example, statistics has become a popular choice for a variety of nonmathematical science majors. In 2005, the American Statistical Association (ASA) released a college report (Aliaga et al., 2005) called the *Guidelines for assessment and instruction in statistical education* (GAISE) and followed up that report in 2016 (GAISE College Report ASA Revision Committee, 2016).

These reports had profound impacts on the teaching of introductory statistics that focus on six objectives: (1) teach statistical thinking, (2) focus on conceptual understanding, (3) integrate real data with context and purpose, (4) foster active learning, (5) use technology to explore concepts and analyze data, and (6) use assessment to improve and evaluate student learning.

College-Wide Curricula Reform Efforts

Thus far, in this section, we have focused on curricula reform efforts that mostly impact specific mathematical courses. Davidson (2017) highlights some college-wide curricula reform efforts that align to many of our core assumptions. For example, Davidson (2017) discusses how Duke has transformed the general education curriculum to focus on complex problems spanning five areas: (1) brain and society; (2) information, society, and culture; (3) global health; (4) education and human development; and (5) energy.

The University of Virginia has transformed its curriculum to focus on (1) aesthetics, (2) empirical and scientific ways of knowing, (3) cultural differences, and (4) ethical questions (Davidson, 2017). There are other examples as well of colleges making some much needed changes.

It is promising to see flagship institutions and large four-year colleges implement innovative changes. Community colleges often lead change but are tied to the university curricula if they desire course equivalencies and seamless transfer opportunities for their students. As Davidson (2017) notes, the rest of higher education has a lot to learn from community colleges who prioritize student growth and have the ability to innovate, as they are not tied to the same ranking system as universities.

The type of changes outlined in this section are necessary as so many students in college gateway mathematics courses are not successful. Davidson (2017) notes that about 60 percent of students enrolled in community college are required to take at least one mathematics course, and about 80 percent of those students never fulfill that requirement. These changes together with corequisite mathematics opportunities are providing some promising results.

COREQUISITE MATHEMATICS

Influenced by the CRAFTY report (Ganter & Haver, 2011) and the crossroads document (American Mathematical Association of Two-Year Colleges, 1995, 2006), the Developmental Mathematics Committee (DMC), appointed by the AMATYC, has been working, since 2009, on reforming the developmental mathematics curriculum (Rotman, n.d.). The DMC created a project they called New Life.

The New Life project proposed pathways allowing students to transition to college-level mathematics courses faster than traditional developmental pathways, with non-STEM students transitioning directly into their college-level courses. The Carnegie Foundation for the Advancement of Teaching, together with the Dana Center at the University of Texas, and a number of community college partners, proposed two new developmental mathematics pathways called Statway and Mathway/Quantway. The work from the New Life project influenced the original development of these pathways (Rotman, n.d.).

Statway and Mathway/Quantway are designed for non-STEM and STEM pathways, respectively. Both pathways allow students to complete credit-bearing mathematics courses in one academic year (with their developmental pathways). The work of these committees formed the foundation for corequisite mathematics projects by proposing pathways utilizing fewer developmental courses. These new pathways are built on the premise that traditional pathways do not adequately prepare the vast majority of students, who never go on to the traditional calculus sequence.

The traditional algebra-intensive sequence, focused on preparing STEM majors, has the wrong goals for non-STEM majors and is a barrier to college success (Cullinane & Treisman, 2010). Thus, corequisite projects typically focus on creating multiple pathways aligned to various meta-majors or AFAs.

What Is Wrong with Traditional Developmental Mathematics?

In 1988, the graduation rate among students who took no remedial-level courses was 57 percent, compared to 29 percent for students who took one or two remedial-level courses, and 19 percent for students who took four remedial-level courses (Kansky, 2008). Adelman (2004) found that the failure rate among the two most widely transferable gateway mathematics courses, college algebra and precalculus, exceeds 50 percent on many campuses.

Approximately 60 percent of community college students across the nation are referred to one or more developmental mathematics courses (Cullinane & Treisman, 2010). Furthermore, approximately 1.7 million students enter college requiring some sort of remediation each year, and nearly one in three recent high school graduates are required to enroll in a remedial course (Complete College America, 2016b).

The profile of the developmental student has evolved from students who have learned the skills but need recall to students who have had content presented but never learned the material and are lacking content and process skills and habits of the mind (Andrusiak, 2018). A synthesis of national research studies provided by Cullinane and Treisman (2010) documents the failure of developmental mathematics across the United States. Cullinane and Treisman (2010) note:

- About two-thirds of developmental mathematics students do not complete their developmental mathematics sequence.
- Success rates decrease as the number of developmental mathematics courses increase.
- The three courses that have the highest rates of failure and withdrawal in postsecondary education are all developmental mathematics courses.
- Developmental mathematics is not an entryway to college-level mathematics success but rather a burial ground.

Nationally, few developmental students graduate or transfer (Complete College America, 2016b). Of two-year students enrolled in developmental courses, 11 percent graduate in three years and 18 percent transfer to four-year institutions within four years (Complete College America, 2016a). Only 20 percent of two-year students, and 36 percent of four-year students, who are enrolled in a developmental course, go on to complete their associated gateway courses (Complete College America, 2016b). In general, the situation is even bleaker for disadvantaged and minority students as shown in figures 3.1 and 3.2.

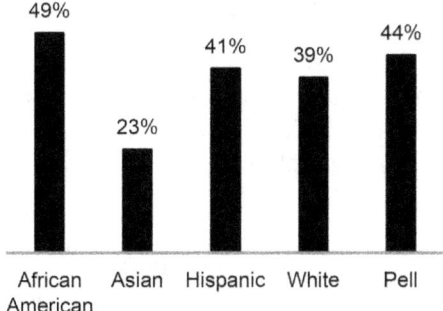

Figure 3.1 Students Enrolled in Remedial Courses at Two-Year Institutions. This figure represents first-time full- and part-time students who started college in fall 2012.

Source: Complete College America (2017).

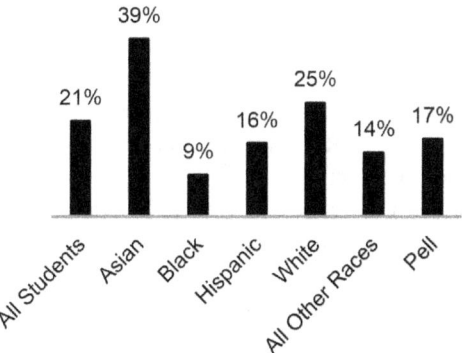

Figure 3.2 Community College Gateway Course Completion by Subgroup. This figure shows the two-year gateway course completion rates for various subgroups who begin in developmental courses.

Source: Complete College America (2016a, 2017).

In New Hampshire, the state of the upcoming case study, currently about 40 percent of all students at two-year institutions require developmental mathematics, with only 24 percent of those students completing an associated gateway mathematics course for degree completion within two years (Complete College America, 2017).

The majority of developmental students succeed in their developmental courses but fail to enroll in the subsequent courses, which often are additional remedial courses (Complete College America, 2016b). Corequisite opportunities leverage these ideas by providing real-time support on the concepts and skills necessary for gateway course success, while reducing the number of remedial courses students engage in to counteract the persistence factor.

Corequisite Mathematics Designs

The basic premise of a corequisite model is to eliminate prerequisite remedial-level courses necessary for gateway course enrollment. This is accomplished by allowing students to enroll directly in their credit-bearing degree completion courses while receiving real-time support. Various corequisite models include:

- co-enrolling in a developmental course and the college-level course;
- enrolling in an additional lab or workshop that meets alongside the college-level course; and
- increasing the number of credits and contact hours for corequisite sections.

Vandal (2017, June 18) outlines many types of models that are often described as corequisite models but fail the previously described premise of corequisite models. These include:

- co-enrolling in two developmental courses at one time;
- delivering academic support in a traditional remedial course;
- co-enrolling in a traditional developmental course that is not aligned with the college-level course; and
- providing academic support in a nontransferable college-level course.

When implemented with fidelity, corequisite models increase success rates from around 20 percent to 60 percent (Vandal, 2017, June 18). By fidelity, Vandal means models that address why traditional remedial-level courses fail. This requires models that not only eliminate the stigma of remedial education but also address the attrition rates attributed to the persistence factor. Additionally, corequisite models must align the content between the corequisite support and the college-level course.

Evaluating Corequisite Mathematics

Much of the criticism associated with the movement toward corequisite mathematics is due to the speed of adoption based upon little-to-no controlled experiments. For example, Goudas (2017) notes that there exists little-to-no accurate and reliable data and rigorous research supporting the effectiveness of corequisite models. The exception being an original corequisite model studied by the Community College Research Center known as the Accelerated Learning Program, and one randomized controlled study (Logue, Watanabe-Rose, & Douglas, 2016) that analyzed the effectiveness of taking an additional structured lab alongside a college-level course.

Additionally, Goudas (2017) notes that more students passing gateway courses is not necessarily resulting in higher graduation rates. In many respects, Goudas is correct. We do not have adequate data to support the success of the corequisite models. As institutions spend more per student, focus deeper on proper placement, support students with more time on tasks, and in general spend more time and energy focused on a model that they want to succeed, we should expect better results.

Education is messy and complex. It is difficult to conduct controlled experiments in educational settings. And Goudas (2017) is correct in the aspect that short-term results might not hold in the long run. However, we have a plethora of data showing that traditional models do not work. Whether we are shifting the focus from graduation goals down to gateway completion goals is not relevant. We are aiming to prepare students for a complex rapidly changing world where they need to be creative and innovative thinkers. Placing students into long remedial sequences results in students leaking from the system (Vandal, 2014).

Engaging in the conversation and focusing on evaluation and change is necessary. Even if corequisite models turn out to not result in long-term success, they are pushing the conversation and focus in new directions, as educators are increasing their commitment to supporting underprepared learners. Perhaps if corequisite models do not have long-term success, educators will be quicker to reevaluate strategies for helping underprepared learners, rather than being complacent as they have been with traditional models for far too many years.

There are many additional concerns. Are students living in the moment of the class and only learning the material for the tests? Will students retain the material in the long run? Can students synthesize the material and use it to solve complex problems? The data show that the vast majority of students who start in developmental courses do not persist in future courses.

Students who are successful in corequisite models go on to additional college-level work and have future opportunities to develop their critical-thinking and problem-solving skills. As Logue (2018) notes, "We can certainly use more information about what specific aspects of co-requisite remediation make it most effective, and for which students. But that is a reason for more research—not cause to favor something worse instead."

The Logue, Watanabe-Rose, and Douglas (2016) study addressed many of the common explanations offered for the success of corequisite models and concerns, including:

- differences in students and selection for remedial and corequisite courses;
- quality of faculty;
- grading;

- differences in mathematical pathways;
- continued success in subsequent courses;
- changing pathways (e.g., from a statistical pathway to a calculus pathway); and
- graduation rates.

In all cases, Logue, Watanabe-Rose, and Douglas (2016) note that the evidence converges on corequisite models being more effective than traditional models. The self-reported data from institutions both large and small, rural and urban, support the success of such models. The particular aspects resulting in the success might not be known. Thus, we should not necessarily jump to any causal relationships.

For example, many assessment and placement measures improperly place students into remedial course work (Vandal, 2014). This improper placement may be partially responsible for lowering gateway completion rates for students who begin in developmental mathematics work. However, study after study seem to show higher course pass rates in corequisite models than in traditional models (Logue, 2018).

CCA (2016b) offers a dynamic website that shows various success models. In many cases, corequisite models result in doubling completion rates of gateway courses for underprepared students (Complete College America, 2016a). Additional information can be found in Vandal (2014). As with any model, unique institutional challenges likely prevent a one-size-fits-all implementation.

Corequisite Mathematics Success—a Case Study

As a case study, consider River Valley Community College (RVCC) in Claremont, New Hampshire. RVCC is a small rural community college in the southwestern part of the state. RVCC serves a population of students from schools that historically score among the lowest in the state on the statewide science and mathematics assessments.

RVCC was hesitant about the success rates being advertised with corequisite models. As Goudas (2017) notes, any intervention in education that doubles success rates seems too good to be true. Furthermore, as a small rural community college, RVCC serves a substantial nontraditional population, and most of the data reported by CCA use metrics on first-time anywhere college students. This excludes a large proportion of the population that have taken at least one college-level course prior to admission.

RVCC spent one academic year researching and designing a model that would eliminate placement exams and barriers into college-level mathematics courses. Using a variety of placement tools, the mathematics department designed placement measures focused on quality advising. They focused on addressing the high attrition rates among developmental students by providing mathematical pathways aligned to students' AFAs. And, they gave students real-time support in meeting the competencies of their gateway courses while allowing students to complete those courses and integrate into their programs of study within one academic year.

RVCC's corequisite model was preceded by a developmental mathematics redesign moving in the direction of corequisite mathematics. In 2012, the mathematics department followed the research of the Statway/Quantway project and created mathematical pathways geared toward AFAs, and opportunities for the vast majority of students to complete their gateway mathematics course within a single academic year (they spent another dedicated year studying the issue). They did this by eliminating one developmental course for the vast majority of students.

RVCC chose to implement a model which requires underprepared students (i.e., students who do not meet the prerequisite for the college-level course) to attend two fifty-minute workshops per week in addition to their gateway mathematics courses. The workshops focus on underlying skills and concepts necessary for gateway course success, along with the concepts being taught in the gateway courses.

RVCC utilized a combination of instructor support and a software package. The college also implemented a drop-in tutoring center. This was not a controlled experimental design; however, the results have fidelity with those reported by other institutions and the Logue, Watanabe-Rose, and Douglas (2016) study.

Figure 3.3 shows the pass rates of students enrolled in RVCC's lowest-level developmental mathematics courses over various semesters. Prior to 2012, the lowest-level developmental course was called Developmental Mathematics, noted as DM in figure 3.3. After 2012 and before fall 2017, the lowest-level developmental course was called Fundamentals of Mathematical Literacy Part I, noted as FML I in figure 3.3. This course was designed to have fidelity with the Statway/Quantway work and represented the non-STEM pathway course.

As the data in figure 3.3 suggest, the success rates in the developmental course are fairly high. Furthermore, the pass rates show a possible increase after the spring 2012 term. This is when the entry-level developmental course was redesigned, based upon the Statway/Quantway model, to focus more directly on the material necessary for gateway course success.

An analysis of the pass rates for the STEM developmental pathway showed similar results. Consistent with the research, students were passing developmental course work, but either failed to enroll in subsequent mathematics work or pass their gateway courses within two academic years as indicated in figure 3.4.

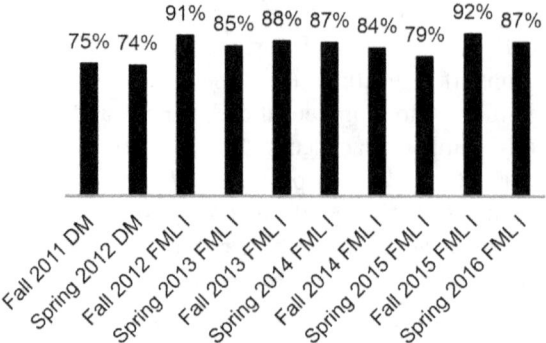

Figure 3.3 Developmental Mathematics Pass Rates. This figure shows the pass rates for students entering the lowest-level developmental course at RVCC between fall semester 2011 and spring semester 2016.

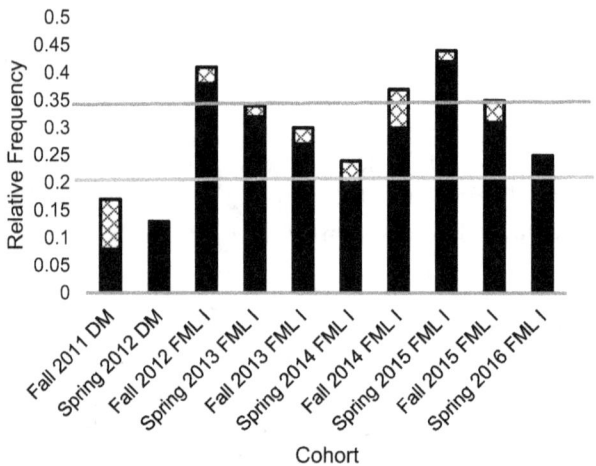

■ Passed GW in 1 Year ▨ Additonal Pass Rate in 2 Years

Figure 3.4 Passed Gateway Mathematics within Two Years by Cohort. This figure shows the gateway mathematics pass rates by cohort between the fall 2011 semester and the spring 2016 semester. The light-gray horizontal line shows the national pass rate, about 20–21%. The dark-gray horizontal line shows the average pass rate at RVCC from fall semester 2012 until spring semester 2016. GW = gateway.

The light-gray horizontal line in figure 3.4 shows the national pass rate referenced earlier (about 20 to 21 percent), and the dark-gray horizontal line shows the average pass rate at RVCC from fall semester 2012 until spring semester 2016. As indicated in figure 3.4, the two-year pass rate at RVCC was lower than the national average prior to the 2012 redesign.

After the 2012 redesign, which eliminated one developmental mathematics course for the vast majority of students, RVCC's average two-year pass rate,

34 percent, exceeded the national average and more than doubled their prior pass rate. However, a 34-percent two-year gateway pass rate is well below the expectations of the mathematics department and college. Thus, beginning in the fall semester of 2017, RVCC implemented the corequisite model explained in the previous section. Figure 3.5 shows the results of all corequisite sections combined, along with the results from the past two academic years captured in figure 3.4 for comparison.

As the data in figure 3.5 indicate, the pass rates are significantly higher after the implementation of corequisite mathematics. A chi-square test of homogeneity was used to determine if there was a statistically significant difference in the pass rates between the spring 2015 cohort (the highest cohort pass rate since the 2012 redesign) and the fall 2017 Functions and Modeling I cohort (the first semester of corequisite mathematics at RVCC and the college algebra course). The test indicated a statistically significant difference in pass rates, $\chi^2 (1, N = 86) = 9.25, p < .01$.

Similar differences exist for the other cohorts. The combined success rates for all corequisite students was 76 percent in fall 2017 and 94 percent in spring 2018. The combined success rates for all students in the same gateway mathematics courses that were placed into the course without the corequisite workshop (i.e., students who met the prerequisite) was 78 percent in fall 2017 and 86 percent in spring 2018.

The success rates for corequisite students are more than double the two-year success rates of students who begin in developmental mathematics,

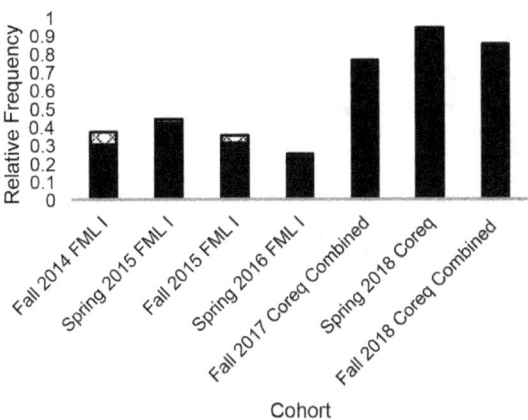

■ Passed GW in One Year ▣ Additonal Pass Rate in Two Years

Figure 3.5 Passed Gateway Mathematics within Two Years by Cohort. This figure shows the gateway mathematics pass rates by cohort between the fall 2014 semester and the fall 2018 semester. GW = gateway.

and corequisite students have combined gateway course pass rates equivalent to non-corequisite students. This is quite amazing considering that corequisite students have previously been placed into developmental courses and assessed as not meeting the prerequisites for college-level success.

In addition to collecting data on success rates, at the end of the fall 2017 and spring 2018 semesters, RVCC surveyed both instructors and students on the ways and extent to which corequisite mathematics was meeting the needs of students. The average student response rate was 67 percent, and there was a 100 percent instructor response rate. RVCC performed a quantitative analysis on five constructs as indicated in figure 3.6. The constructs represented whether students and instructors believed that corequisite mathematics was providing sufficient time, flexibility, tutoring support, and connections to college-level work to achieve college-level success.

Mann–Whitney U tests were run on all five constructs to determine if the perceived extent to which corequisite mathematics was meeting the needs of students differed by instructor or student opinion. The null hypothesis tests whether the distributions of the two groups are equal, whereas the alternative hypothesis tests the differences in mean ranks (if the distributions have

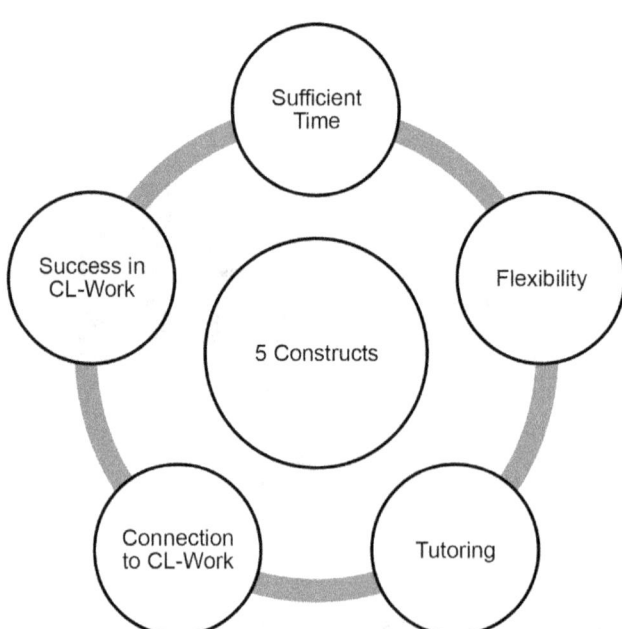

Figure 3.6 Constructs Assessed on Survey. This figure shows the five constructs assessed on instructor and students surveys. CL = college level.

different shapes) or the differences in medians (if the distributions have the same shape).

In all five cases, results were not statistically significant. The data from surveys of instructors and corequisite students revealed no difference in the perception of the ways and extent to which corequisite mathematics is meeting the needs of students, and, generally, the perception on all five categories was positive.

In addition to the quantitative analysis, an open-response question was created allowing both instructors and students to provide additional feedback on the corequisite model. All statements from both instructors and students were coded and analyzed for themes. Both instructors and students pointed to common themes.

Both students and instructors cited too heavy of an emphasis on the use of the software package. They expressed the desire for labs to focus on the flexible help students needed in real time for gateway course success and cited that skill practice using the software package could occur outside of lab times. In general, both instructors and students were grateful for the opportunity to take corequisite courses. As one instructor said:

> It was very clear to me that my Stats students who were in the coreq labs did benefit greatly from that experience. All but one of them is on track to pass the course with at least a B for their final grade. The one exception is a student who has missed several classes due to a significant medical problem and will probably take a grade of Incomplete.

From a qualitative perspective, many students articulated the value of the workshops and expressed their gratefulness for the support that they felt from both lecture and lab instructors as captured by this student's statement:

> I am thankful for the opportunity to be a part of this lab class, combined with Functions & Modeling I. Without this new structure, I would have not been eligible to participate in the class without first taking additional refresher courses, at much more expense and time in school. I feel like the lab is a good idea for those of us that need it. I feel like it could be structured a little differently though. I feel that lab should be more like a reinforcement for what we are currently doing in class, along with doing the fundamental (software) supplement, as needed.

There were a number of limitations to the study. As noted earlier, this was not an experimental design. Random assignment for the chi-square test was not possible. There was potential voluntary response bias to the survey. Only a single question was used for each construct (to keep the survey simple and quick). Some students in corequisite courses came through RVCC's previous developmental course sequence.

However, the initial assessment has fidelity with results being achieved at other institutions and those presented by Logue, Watanabe-Rose, and Douglas (2016). Furthermore, both students and instructors expressed positive perceptions regarding the ways and extent to which the program is meeting students' needs.

The particular aspects of the RVCC model contributing to student success might not yet be known; however, the model is heading in the right direction. And, even if one does not buy into corequisite models, what is clear is that the traditional pathways do not work. Thus, new models need to be developed and tested. Furthermore, success rates are only one piece of the puzzle.

Educators need to ensure that students are developing the critical-thinking and problem-solving skills that will allow them to develop into creative and innovative thinkers who can solve novel problems in a global environment. Students do not learn these skills by memorizing facts and procedures for exams. The momentum and traction gained by merging gateway reform efforts and corequisite models can be leveraged to focus on assessment reform.

The majority of gateway courses are students' first and last experiences with college-level mathematics. If the majority of students take a single college-level mathematics course, do we want them memorizing skills, facts, and procedures for an exam or applying those in complex situations connected to their majors and future careers?

Students have not been receiving the appropriate levels of support in gateway courses. Furthermore, the heavy emphasis on exams and quizzes as primary assessment measures is causing student disillusionment with mathematics and degrading their attitudes toward mathematics.

Even in a highly technological era, students still question the value of mathematics. Sitting for exams and quizzes with no access to resources mimics almost no real-world situations students will engage in when they enter the workforce. Eliminating exams in gateway courses in favor of inquiry-based collaborative learning focused on projects aligned to students' majors, talents, and passions will increase student engagement and motivation while building the skills students need to succeed in a global society.

ASSESSMENT TRANSFORMATION

The reform curricula models presented within this chapter provide guidance on assessment practices. For example, the GAISE College Report ASA Revision Committee framework (GAISE, 2016) lists a variety of formative and summative assessment options such as homework, quizzes, exams, projects, activities, oral presentations, written reports, minute papers, and article critiques. The framework also contains a variety of sample assessment items. The AMATYC (2006) lists assessment as one of the most important professional responsibilities of a mathematics educator. The AMATYC discusses the assessment implementation cycle, which is shown in figure 3.7.

This section focuses on assessment at the classroom level, that is, those assessments that involve individual instructors assessing individual students and their progress on learning outcomes. Classroom-level assessment involves instructor-developed tools as a means to inform learning and adapt instruction to meet the individual needs of all students.

Assessment used as a means for improving instruction and student outcomes, rather than focused on students' weaknesses, can have a positive impact on student behavior and performance (AMATYC, 2006). However, as Davidson (2017) notes much of the assessment of our current educational system is based upon late nineteenth- and early twentieth-century standards built upon the development of standardized tests, IQ tests, grades, and statistics based upon a normal curve.

Education needs a revolution in every classroom. What we teach, how we teach, and how we assess student learning should facilitate students taking charge of their own learning, collaborating in new ways, learning to

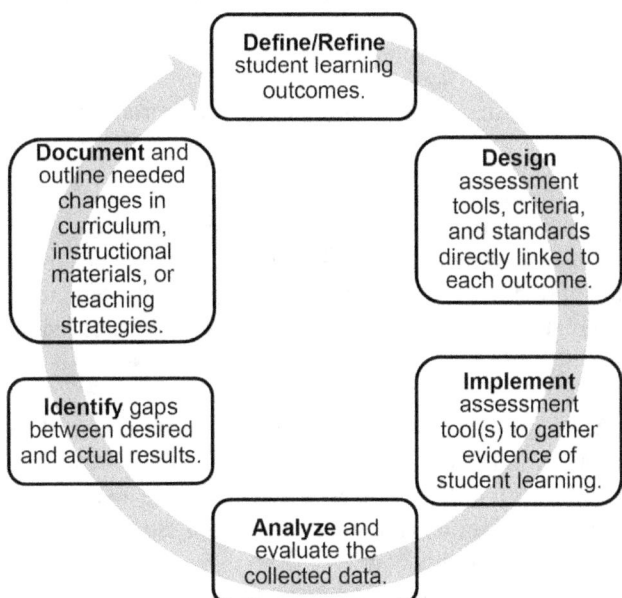

Figure 3.7 The Assessment Implementation Cycle. This figure shows the AMATYC (2006) assessment cycle.

Source: AMATYC (2006).

respond to feedback, and becoming independent learners. Within the New Life framework, Rotman (n.d.) notes that the model calls for us to modernize our instruction and assessment by integrating a variety of teaching methods, using diverse technology, and assessing student learning in deeper ways.

Rotman (n.d.) also states that changing the content and methodology is not enough: "If we can revolutionize our colleges and universities so that we do not teach to the test but rather challenge and empower students, we will do the best possible job helping them to succeed in an uncertain world" (as cited in Davidson, 2017, p. 14). Jenkins and Fink (2018) point to research supporting the conclusion that colleges should be making every effort to integrate active learning opportunities into introductory courses.

Active learning opportunities are associated with better academic outcomes, increasing student motivation and persistence in their programs, and fostering a sense of confidence in students in their abilities to learn and gain momentum in their fields of interest (Jenkins & Fink, 2018). Eliminating exams from gateway mathematics courses is a small change in classroom assessment that has the potential for dramatic long-term impacts.

Skills and concepts can be assessed through formative assessments and problem-sets (or even quizzes as a transition), and exams can be replaced with student-choice projects that align to students' majors and talents. The costs of continuing to overemphasize summative assessments are too great to continue to sustain.

Summative Assessment, Attitudes, and Mathematics Trauma

As Davidson (2017) noted, summative assessments have long dominated education and have a history tied to standardized assessments. The No Child Left Behind era served to further strengthen the reliance on summative assessments in order to prepare students for high-stakes standardized testing. Educators knew that the expectations of No Child Left Behind were unrealistic, and that the mandates ignored some of the real issues facing education such as poverty and segregation (Ravitch, 2016).

Ravitch (2016) documents the clear failure of the mandates of the No Child Left Behind Act and the overreliance on high-stakes standardized exams. It is well known that standardized assessments are single measurements in time and are subject to variation. Those who develop these assessments would be the first to describe them this way.

The performance on exams can be impacted by the breakfast a student had or did not have on a particular day, the emotional stability of their home life and relationships, daily stress, and a number of other factors. Yet we still insist on weighting these exams heavily in our college courses. Most adults, who are exhibiting high levels of success in their careers, would have difficulty passing many of the standardized exams their children are completing (Ravitch, 2016).

Black et al. (2003) worked with groups of teachers to integrate formative assessment into their classrooms and practices. They describe how difficult it was to get teachers to not focus on summative assessments, as that focus is so engrained into the culture of education. In fact, the teachers themselves developed strategies for the formative use of summative assessments as they saw summative assessments as an integral part of the assessment process (Black et al., 2003).

School does a good job of preparing students for more school. Neuroscience research makes it clear that practice makes permanent (Sousa, 2017). Summative assessments encourage the memorization of facts and procedures that students are unlikely to recall a month or two after completing a course, if they do not have the opportunity to practice those skills.

Most of us likely work jobs where it is important to consult a variety of resources to accomplish complex tasks (e.g., consulting research articles, books, technology, and human capital). To ignore those resources would not only be inefficient but also be counterproductive to accomplishing the tasks at hand.

Davidson (2017) notes how schools create environments that do not mimic real-life situations, as we often do not allow students to use important resources on summative assessments. Additionally, mathematics educators need to consider the impact of these exams on students' emotional states, and whether they are counterproductive to the core values outlined in this chapter. This is particularly important for developmental mathematics students who bring fragile emotional dispositions to their mathematical experiences.

Students' Attitudes and Assessment

The study of attitudes has its origin in social psychology. Even though there is a plethora of research on students' attitudes toward mathematics, the study of attitudes in mathematics remains relevant as attitudes are associated with performance (Aiken, 1976; Choi & Chang, 2011; Di Martino & Zan, 2010; Hattie, 2009; Idil, Narli, & Aksoy, 2016; Ma & Kishor, 1997; McLeod, 1992; Wilkins & Ma, 2003). Furthermore, mathematics self-beliefs impact students' life decisions, educational choices, beliefs about their abilities as learners of mathematics, and career choices (Organisation for Economic Co-operation and Development [OECD], 2013).

Research has shown that mathematics attitudes are relatively stable over time (e.g., McLeod, 1992; Wilkins & Ma, 2003). However, more recent research has shown that students' attitudes can and do shift over time

(Andrusiak, 2018; Di Martino & Zan, 2010). Additionally, research has shown that middle school is a pivotal time in the formation of attitudes toward mathematics (Mullis et al., 2012).

There is little-to-no research on the microvariables (those that can be controlled by teachers on a day-to-day basis) impacting students' attitudes toward mathematics, as the majority of the research is focused on macrovariables (e.g., parents' attitudes, teachers' attitudes, instructional approaches, peer support, and gender) that impact attitudes (Andrusiak, 2018). The lack of theoretical clarity on the construct of attitudes is attributed to conflicting findings in the research on the variables impacting attitudes, and their connections to achievement in mathematics (Belbase, 2013; Di Martino & Zan, 2003, 2010; Eleftherios & Theodosius, 2007; Hattie, 2009; Idil, Narli, & Aksoy, 2016; Ma & Kishor, 1997; McLeod, 1992).

This lack of clarity has resulted in a call for a greater emphasis on research focused on the construct of attitudes (Di Martino & Zan, 2003, 2010; Goldin et al., 2016). Using a grounded theory approach, Di Martino and Zan (2010) developed a theoretical three-dimensional model for students' attitudes toward mathematics.

The model contains eight different attitude profiles across three dimensions: (1) an emotional dimension; (2) a perceived competence dimension; and (3) an understanding of mathematics dimension. Moreover, Di Martino and Zan (2010) proposed using attitudes as a construct for the observer to understand the intentional actions of individuals, rather than inherent qualities of students. This represented an important shift in the study of attitudes toward mathematics.

Andrusiak (2018) addressed the lack of research on microvariables impacting students' attitudes toward mathematics, the call for a greater focus on the construct of attitudes, and the identification of middle school as a pivotal time in attitude formation. In 2018, Andrusiak conducted a study with sixth- and seventh-grade students, using the Experience Sampling Method (ESM) (Larson & Csikszentmihalyi, 1983), to test Di Martino and Zan's (2010) model in real time.

The ESM captures random representative moments in time, by sending signals to students in real time triggering a response. In Andrusiak's (2018) study, the response was filling out a journal protocol, aligned to Di Martino and Zan's (2010) framework. The journals captured, as described by students, the real-time classroom factors impacting students' attitudes toward mathematics. Seventy-five students participated in the study, 477 random classroom moments were captured, and 3,988 student statements were analyzed and coded.

Tests and quizzes dominated the classroom activities within all four attitude profiles that represent a negative emotional reaction toward mathematics.

These emotional reactions are not only counterproductive to the core assumptions outlined in this chapter but also counterproductive to addressing the future needs of the STEM workforce. The Business Higher Education Forum (2011) found that less than one-third of college-bound high school seniors expressed interest in STEM fields, and of those interested in STEM fields, less than 20 percent demonstrated proficiency in mathematics.

Ruef (2018) describes mathematics trauma as the worst manifestation of mathematics anxiety, resulting in a mental shutdown. This is consistent with neuroscience research and the impact of emotions on learning. Students must feel both physically safe and emotionally secure before learning can occur (Sousa, 2017). Students' emotional reactions can either support or inhibit their learning of mathematics, with strong negative emotional reactions resulting in the avoidance of new learning situations and anxiety.

Ruef (2018) notes how both educators and parents maintain antiquated ideas about what it means to be good at mathematics. Often those ideas as associated with speed and accuracy. This results in an overreliance on timed tests which create fear and shut down students' working memories (Ruef, 2018). Moreover, feedback on summative assessments is often delayed. This results in only the best students enjoying the privilege of experiencing or feeling success (Christensen, Horn, & Johnson, 2011).

A Call to Action

There is lack of evidence that exams have fidelity with the core values outlined in this chapter. If we are going to prepare students to think critically and develop novel solutions to complex problems in a rapidly changing global economy, while valuing individual talents, it is time for exams to make an exit (or at least move back from center stage) from entry-level mathematics courses. Eliminating exams not only frees up instructional time but also creates space for more meaningful assessments and project-based inquiry-focused learning opportunities.

Educators can create open projects that allow students to explore areas of interest while showcasing their talents. Open projects are projects that are not already designed by the instructor and scripted to have particular solutions to defined problems. Students define their own research questions that aim to solve meaningful problems. In doing so, students develop their own projects that seek to build connections between the content of the course and their majors or other interests.

Teachers should provide students with project guidelines outlining expectations, including a timeline for various project components that allows for formative feedback, and clear details on how students will be assessed. Well-written rubrics provide guidance for students and mitigate teachers' concerns regarding the time commitment necessary to grade projects (especially for large classes). Teachers can also require students to detail how their projects connect to course competencies, and students should reflect on their own learning.

In allowing open projects, teachers are also modeling taking risks and problem-solving strategies as students are not working on problems that teachers have already solved. Schoenfeld (1983) describes how mathematics educators do a poor job modeling the problem-solving process. Students rarely have the opportunity to see their teachers engage in true problem-solving, as teachers are engaged in solving problems with students for which they have already worked out the solutions. This creates a false impression that mathematics teachers do not engage in productive struggle while working on mathematics.

Some examples of student-proposed projects from three different courses the author recently taught include conducting experiments to examine bacterial logistic growth patterns and isolate growth phase shifts; examining sound pressure level decay by building, testing, and using distributed mode loudspeakers; analyzing publicly available data to look for relationships between the strengths of hurricanes and their points of origin; looking at the science behind intoxication and how alcohol is processed by the body; examining the brachistochrone problem; and calculating the avalanche runout distance in Tukerman Ravine on Mount Washington, in New Hampshire.

In chapter 6, Carlton J. Fitzgerald and Simona Laurian-Fitzgerald described strategies for immersing students in complex projects. They discuss the importance of groups attending to both academic and social goals and various elements of cooperative learning. It is important to gradually increase the complexity of projects while moving students from dependent learners to independent learners. Multiple projects over the course of a semester afford such opportunities.

Eliminating exams does not equate with devaluing skills and procedures. Skills and procedures can be assessed through problem-sets, portfolios, self-reflection, journals, the use of technology, and a variety of other techniques. For example, the MAA has a free online problem-set tool where instructors can choose a variety of individualized problems, written by other professors, to assign to students. The tool also allows professors to modify existing problems or create their own.

Not all students need to learn the same material in the same time. Eliminating exams opens up greater opportunities for student collaboration while creating a community of learners. Students need ample opportunities to generate their own research questions, explore what they believe is impossible, and work on solutions to complex problems. How much longer can we "afford" to consume valuable learning opportunities with timed tests?

CONCLUSIONS

There is ample evidence that traditional developmental mathematics pathways are creating a barrier to student success rather than a bridge. While there is no sufficient scientific evidence of the success of the recent corequisite mathematical reform movement, initial positive results are being replicated across the nation and across both small and large institutions, rural and urban.

Increasing the percentage of students who are successful in entry-level gateway mathematics courses is a positive outcome of the corequisite reform movement. However, this change alone is not sufficient to guarantee that students develop the critical-thinking and problem-solving skills required to be successful in a rapidly changing global society.

Education is frequently reformed. Past reformations have failed to address the late nineteenth- and early twentieth-century standards that our current educational system is based upon—including the use of testing and exams as the major form of assessment in our classrooms. These testing situations mimic almost no real-world situations students will engage in when they enter the workforce and seem to satisfy no one except testing companies and politicians.

Educational neuroscience supports that we all learn at different rates and in different ways. Schools and colleges have done well in preparing students for more school. There is sufficient research to support thinking about assessment in nontraditional ways. An overreliance on exams is degrading students' emotional states toward mathematics. Educators are implicitly supporting methodologies counterproductive to increasing interest in STEM fields.

Students who explore their passions and talents through open projects build critical-thinking and problem-solving skills while seeing the relevancy that mathematics plays in their lives. It is time for education to be transformed. It is time we value every student and recognize that success looks different for each student. It is time for educators and students to retake control of education.

Eliminating exams from all gateway mathematics courses is a transformational change in how we think about and view assessment. This change has the potential for sustained benefits for all students and can begin in any classroom today.

Chapter 4

Every Child Must Be Valued

Amanda Bastoni

Rita Pierson, in her 2013 TED Talk, said, "Every child deserves a champion, an adult who will never give up on them, who understands the power of connection, and insists that they become the best that they can possibly be" (7:13). Her message went viral almost immediately, electrifying both the live audience and the education world. Although Pierson died shortly after speaking, her presentation was filled with such passion, conviction, and truth that it continues to be one of the most watched TED Talks of all time. Her TED Talk has been translated into forty-seven different languages and has had more than 9 million views. Pierson's message was revolutionary and simple—every child is valuable. Every. Single. One.

This concept is the structure, the foundation, and the baseline that must inform any attempt at reimagining what a new educational system should look like. This is the core philosophical shift that must be made first. Before talking about how to develop students with globalization skills, or spending time trying to improve mathematics scores, educators must commit to the fundamental belief that *every* child deserves a champion because *every* child is valuable. If this were to happen, if the educational world decided that all children—those living in poverty, those learning English, those who had aptitudes for hands-on learning, those whose parents were in jail—were equally valuable, everything would change. Every. Single. Thing.

Diversity is itself valuable. Take the "Doomsday Vault" in Norway, for example. Down a long tunnel, deep within the permafrost are millions of seeds from every country—India, Britain, Mexico, Syria—a worldwide collection of crops. Many people believe that these seeds are kept for post-apocalyptic purposes, in case a catastrophic event wiped out civilization and the world needed to grow food again. Cary Fowler, the man considered the "father" of the seed vault sees it differently. He describes it as a safety deposit box, "a backup drive" to safeguard against the lack of diversity in today's crops (as cited in Ramsey, 2017). The issue for biologists is that a lack of diversity leads to susceptibility to disease.

But diversity is not just important in the plant world. Industry leaders strive for diversity in the workplace because diversity means new ideas, and new ideas lead to more creative teams, which ultimately increase the bottom line. *Forbes* magazine reports that inclusive diverse teams make "better business decisions 87% of the time" (as cited in Lawson, 2017). Think about voice recognition, for example. When devices and apps such as Alexa or Siri were first launched, women reported having a hard time communicating with them. Women tried speaking louder. They enunciated. Nothing helped.

These devices just could not hear them. That is because the issue was hardwired. These systems were created by men and thus recognized men's voices significantly better (Reynolds, 2017). The designers and engineers who created these devices lacked diversity and made an inferior product because of it.

Education needs to recognize this message: diversity matters. Studies show students perform better in classes where the teacher looks like they do. Unfortunately, for students of color and boys, most teachers are white females. In fact, "77 percent of teachers in public and private elementary and high schools are women" (Miller, 2018, para. 4) and 80 percent of the teachers are white (Mehta & Fine, 2019). According to Seth Gershenson (as cited in Miller, 2018), an economist studying education policy at American University, these are large hurdles to overcome.

On an even more basic level, diversity in the classroom is necessary in order to accomplish the primary goals of education: the learning of new things. The very act of learning relies on being confronted with new information, weighing that information against what is already known, and then potentially forming a new opinion. Therefore, unless a student meets someone with a new idea or is forced to engage with someone who has a different life experience, they cannot learn.

Diversity is essential to survival, success, and learning, yet education narrowly defines the kind of intelligence it values and thus the kinds of students it invests in. This narrow way of looking at the talent pool leaves out many students and results in a problematic lack of diversity.

Frank McCourt was born very poor. He left school at the age of thirteen, yet he spent twenty-seven years teaching in the New York Public Schools, retired, and wrote best-selling books. Maya Angelou dropped out of school in her teens but went on to write poetry and novels, which are celebrated around the world. Hillary Swank, Whoopi Goldberg, Richard Branson (Virgin Records and Airlines), Houdini, Ray Kroc (turned McDonalds into the world's largest fast-food chain), Elton John, Walt Disney also all dropped out of high school. Other famous and successful people like Bill Gates, Mark Zuckerberg, Oprah Winfrey, and Lady Gaga, all dropped out of college.

Did these individuals go on to be successful, despite the fact that the education system did not celebrate their abilities? Were they successful in life even though they were not successful in school?

The answer to both of those questions is, yes. But, how many students like Angelou and Branson were not? *In outliers: The story of success*, Malcom Gladwell (2008) explains it this way:

> We are so caught in the myths of the best and the brightest and the self-made that we think outliers spring naturally from the earth. We look at the young Bill Gates and marvel that our world allowed that thirteen-year-old to become a fabulously successful entrepreneur. But that is the wrong lesson. Our world only allowed one thirteen-year-old unlimited access to a time sharing terminal in 1968. If a million teenagers had been given the same opportunity, how many more Microsofts would we have today? (p. 268)

Today, the education system values one thing above all else—getting into college. High school students are taught that the path to success starts with doing well in high school—taking Advanced Placement (AP) tests, getting good grades, getting good SAT scores—all to get into a four-year college. The idea is this: do well in school so you can do well in subsequent schooling. Why are educators surprised then when industry professionals claim that students are not prepared to get jobs? Students have not been prepared to work. They have been prepared to go to school.

This is not what the world or students need. Employers report they need workers who can analyze problems and generate solutions, who can communicate with clients and work as a team, and who can use new technology and teach others to be successful. Employers need employees who can show up to work on time and who can do what it takes to get the job done. As Mehta and Fine, wrote in their 2019 book, *In search of deeper learning*: "Schools will need to do their part to develop skilled, creative, educated, informed, and empathetic citizens and leaders—the kind of people that our economy, society, and democracy demand" (p. 12). The world needs students who know how the three branches of government work and it needs students who can analyze beautiful poetry, but it also needs students who can get a job and survive after their formal education is complete.

In 2015, First Lady, Michelle Obama, looked out at an audience gathered at the South Court Auditorium and told them about her vision for education. Her message included valuing every student, not just those headed to a four-year college. Instead of calling for more rigorous testing or praising academic success, Mrs. Obama commended the work of Career and Technical

Education (CTE) centers. She expressed support of programs once referred to as vocational, which include courses such as automotive, culinary, manufacturing, and electricity. Each of these courses give students hands-on learning experiences, internship opportunities, and certifications while in high school.

Mrs. Obama (2015) demonstrated that she valued all pathways to success when she spoke against the stigma that so often accompanies the trades:

> We're here because we want to make sure that you get all the skills and the tools that you need to reach your dreams. And those dreams are amazing and they're big and they're huge, so you need all the support you can get. We're here because we know that one of the best ways to do that is through career and technical education—CTE. And I don't know how many people know about CTE, but more people should because in today's world, a high school diploma just is not enough. . . . If you want to learn cutting-edge skills, if you want to prepare yourself for college and a good career, if you want to go into the culinary arts . . . or start your own business, or work in a hospital, or go into 3D printing—whatever it is, it's important for students to realize that a four-year university is not the only option. (paras. 6–8)

Two Harvard researchers, Jal Mehta and Sarah Fine (2019), spent six years examining thirty schools across the United States. They conducted interviews, watched classrooms, and spoke to students. Mehta and Fine (2019) found that the learning happening in the "peripheral" classes and in extracurricular experiences was "more vital than the core" (p. 252).

Mehta and Fine (2019) found that theater, sports, and CTE experiences facilitated the key ingredients for "deeper learning" such as relevance, community, and choice, often lacking in core academic classes. The "peripheral" experiences provided made students "active producers rather than passive recipients" (Mehta & Fine, 2019, p. 252) and provided "interaction with different skill levels rather than tracking" (p. 252).

In 2016, the Thomas B. Fordham Institute followed three cohorts of more than 100,000 students in Arkansas (as cited in Dougherty, 2016). The results were significant. The more CTE courses a student took, the greater their likelihood of graduating from high school and the higher their probability of being employed.

So why are students not enrolling in CTE more? David Etzwiler, CEO of the Siemens Foundation explains: "There is a perception problem in promoting vocational education—or Career Technical Education, as we call it in the United States—and it's hurting our students and our society" (as cited in Falzon, 2017, para. 9).

If CTE is good for the economy and good for students, why is there a "perception problem?" One word: value. The education system still does not value all career pathways or choices. Until recently, the educational system has linked vocational careers with the term blue collar and insinuated that these kind of careers are less valuable, less successful, and less desirable. When attending a four-year college is elevated as the measure of success, the education system makes a value judgment. The message to parents and students is that aptitudes and abilities are not as important to success as acquiring a four-year degree.

The educational system does this both covertly and overtly. For instance, across the country many CTE courses, such as biotechnology, allow students to earn high school and college credit at the same time. To receive this status, the high school class, teacher, and curriculum are evaluated with the same rigorous standards as any college class. If the high school class meets the qualifications, it is designated as a dual-enrollment course and students are awarded transferable college credits.

Despite this designation and the requirements needed, CTE classes in most high schools are still weighted less in GPA calculations than AP credits in similar courses. A student in a dual-enrollment class is guaranteed to receive college credit if they earn a passing grade, but a student who completes an AP course must first pass the AP test before they can receive credit.

According to the AP score distribution for 2019 (Total Registration, 2017–2019), 70.8 percent of students received a score of 3 or less on the AP Biology test. Most colleges will only award credit if a student earns a 4 or a 5. In AP English Literature and Composition, only 21.1 percent of students earned a 4 or a 5.

Yet students in these AP classes, even those who do not receive a high enough score on the AP test to earn college credit are receiving more weight on their final GPA score, than students in CTE classes. It is also difficult to understand why most states do not have graduation requirements around CTE classes or internships but do have graduation requirements for physical education and art.

Even CTE teachers are less valued as educators. For example, despite two-thirds of states in the United States reporting a shortage of CTE teachers in at least one specialty area, the majority of states do not count years of working in the field, as equal to years of teaching. This means, for example, that an electrical teacher with thirty years of invaluable field experience would start teaching and be paid the same as a twenty-something teacher who has no experience and is just starting their career.

CTE teachers are expected to have significant advanced skills but are not rewarded for it by the education system. The problem with undervaluing some classes, experiences, pathways, or careers, is that it leads to not valuing the students who chose them.

In the 1980s, after the publication of *A nation at risk* (The National Commission on Excellence in Education, 1983, April), the United States shifted the focus of education away from job training and toward a more narrow view of what success looked like. As a society, the United States decided to stop valuing pathways that led directly to careers, and, afraid they were being surpassed by other countries, decided that inequities in race, gender, and income could be overcome if every child went to college.

Today:

> As a result of the curriculum reforms since 1983, there is no longer much room for career preparation in high school. For instance, an average of 22 of the 26 credits required for a high-school degree are reserved for academic courses. (Carnevale, Hanson, & Fasules, 2018)

The problem is, college is not an end point. Students who have spent years being prepared to do well in school are not necessarily ready to go into the working world. Not only that, but the presumed goal of sending students to college to ensure success and overcome inequities is a fallacy.

"Less than half of young adults in the United States earn a bachelor's degree, associate degree, or industry-recognized certificate post-secondary credential" (Carnevale, Hanson, & Fasules, 2018). And the system is rigged. Students who are accepted into Ivy League schools are still more likely to be white and wealthy and to have parents who are alumni. *The Washington Post* found that children of alumni had a "45 percent greater chance of admissions (across the top 30 schools in the United States) than other applicants" (Selingo, 2017, para. 5).

The Upshot reported that at thirty-eight colleges in America, including five in the Ivy League, "more students came from the top 1% of the income scale than from the entire bottom 60%" (Aisch et al., 2017, para. 2). Essentially, telling students they are only valuable if they go to college, and they are more valuable if they go to an elite college, is not only setting them up for failure, since many will not go and many will dropout, but it is also placing value in an unfair system. "Even though most lower-income students fare well at elite colleges, there are relatively few of them there" (Aisch et al., 2017, para. 17).

It all boils down to value.

Brene Brown (2017), PhD and *The New York Times* best-selling author, gives some clues to the work it would take to really change the education system so that all children are valued. In her book, *Braving the wilderness* (2017), she said:

> We are going to need to intentionally be with people who are different from us. We're going to have to sign up, join, and take a seat at the table. We're going to have to learn how to listen, have hard conversations, look for joy, share pain, and be more curious than defensive. (p. 37)

Doing this will be hard work because making this kind of philosophical shift will not be a one-and-done change, and there is no end of the year test to give that will prove success. It is hard to imagine a politician going to touring the country with a sign on the side of their campaign bus that reads: "Let's create schools where every child and every ability is valued."

The first step to reform, truly reform education, is to decide, as an educational system, that *all* students, whether they intend to get a two-year degree, a four-year degree, or an industry-certified credential are valuable and will be educated with equal passion and commitment. Like Pierson (2013) said, every student must be seen as a contributing member of society capable of productivity. We must value them all. Every. Single. One.

ALL FEELINGS MUST BE VALUED

Recently, a local New England school board voted to allow the school's Junior Reserve Officers' Training Corps (JROTC) program to start a pellet gun club and practice on the school grounds. Hearing this news, sixty students demanded to meet with school administrators to express their concerns. These students supported the pellet club and the JROTC program, but they were against hosting the program on the school campus, especially since there was a local shooting range one mile down the road willing to host the club for free.

"We are afraid. It's hard to go to school," said students. Over and over again they tried to explain where they were coming from saying things like, "We know pellet guns can't hurt us, but we don't want to normalize guns on school campuses." The adults in the room seemed perplexed. They shook their heads and fired off facts about the safety of pellet guns. Some of the adults thought students just needed more exposure to guns or even training on how to identify a real gun. Others called the students' fears "illogical" and insinuated they were overreacting. So many adults did not see the connection between the students' fears and an inability to learn.

This is a problem.

In a world where students and teachers are coming to work afraid, the solution is not to ignore the problem or downplay the feelings, the solution is to value all feelings.

In *Visible learning*, John Hattie (2012) found that one of the biggest ways a teacher can impact learning is to create "classroom cohesion." Hattie found that in classrooms where students and teachers get along and where all students feel supported and united in the goal of learning, they *all* did better. Despite age, ethnicity, gender, or academic standing, everybody, it turns out, learns better when they have positive relationships with those around them (Hattie, 2012, p. 103).

Educators refer to a teacher's ability to create cohesion and reduce disruption as their classroom management skills. As education writer Matthew A. Kraft explained in his 2010 article, "From ringmaster to conductor," "No amount of dedication, lesson planning, or content knowledge is sufficient to compensate for ineffective classroom and behavior management techniques that result in discordant learning environments. Effective teaching and learning can take place only in harmonious learning environments" (p. 45).

Classroom management includes the development of relationships, the establishment of community, and a commitment to teamwork, but it starts with safety. To learn, people must feel safe (Hammond & Jackson, 2015). This concept is rooted in biology. When humans do not feel safe, a biological mechanism kicks in and their brains are hijacked by the amygdala (the animal base part of the brain that has nothing to do with thought and only cares about keeping itself alive).

In order to take over, the amygdala floods the brain with cortisol, and it immediately goes into safety mode—"fight, flight, freeze, or appease" (Hammond & Jackson, 2015, p. 40). This system allows humans to react really quickly to danger, which is incredibly good for surviving something like a zombie apocalypse but is really bad for learning. Cortisol stops learning. In effect, when danger is near, the brain says, "Guys we are in trouble. Stop everything. No more digesting. No more thinking. Nothing else matters, until we can get to higher ground and feel safe again."

Another safety mechanism in the human brain is being attuned to the emotions of other humans close by. It is like emotions are biologically catching. If one student in the classroom gets emotionally hijacked, if their brain starts to flood with cortisol because they feel unsafe, then those around them are more likely to go into flight-or-fight mode too. Thus, when one student is disengaged or resistant, others will become distracted and potentially disengaged as well (Hammond & Jackson, 2015, p. 66).

What kinds of things cause stress or fear responses in students? The list is long. Feeling incompetent or misunderstood, not getting enough to eat, having parents going through a divorce, not doing well on a quiz in the previous class, having a peer that bullies them sitting a few rows over, not feeling heard or empowered, seeing their peers walking around with fake guns, and so on. Another major source of stress for many students comes from the value placed by the educational system on final exams. When 15 percent of a final grade is attributed to the score on a final exam, students who are overachieving and have multiple commitments and pressures, as well as students from marginalized communities dealing with food insecurities, all feel increased levels of anxiety. Many of the students who experience stress from just coming to school hail from marginalized communities. Essentially, the educational system, because of its institutional biases, sets up students for difficulty due to their race, class, language, or gender.

Whatever the reason, it is important to remember that many students are walking into classrooms with their safety-threat detection system already on high alert. These students are "code red," alert for any social, physical, or psychological threats. And, while this may help them survive, it does not help them learn.

So how does the educational system ensure that teachers are creating safe classrooms? Through teacher evaluations, focused on assessing classroom management. The stated goal of most teacher evaluation systems rooted in coaching teachers is to help them learn new effective techniques and to do this through a dialog about best practices. However, at most schools, this is not happening.

> One of the fateful decisions made when creating the American school system was to place power in a small, mostly male, administrative class, rather than to develop the mostly female teaching force as a full-fledged profession. The consequence is that it is hard to draw a talented, capable, and diverse workforce into teaching, which, in turn, only exacerbates the desire for administrative control, perpetuating the downward spiral. (Mehta & Fine, 2019, p. 36)

Added to the problem is a lack of time. Principals and other administrative evaluators just do not have enough time to give meaningful coaching or developmental feedback. They have too many teachers' classrooms to visit, too many forms to fill out, and too many other responsibilities. Despite these flaws, numerous districts have tied evaluations directly to pay and/or to continued job placement.

Some administrators respond to this lack of time by simply giving all teachers average or good scores. Instead of having long, potentially difficult conversations, they choose not to rock the boat. This approach does not help teachers grow. More than one superintendent has started the first fall administrative meetings trying to stop this practice, with some version of the following statement, "We must hold teachers accountable. No teacher should get a perfect score in any area of an observation."

Without mentors or coaches, but with the expectation they must be skilled at classroom management, many teachers report that the evaluation process leaves them feeling judged, mistrusted, confused, upset, stressed, fearful, and unsafe. In other words, teachers are walking into the classroom feeling much like the students—caught in a flight-or-fight mentality.

Teachers leave the profession for a variety of reasons, but a 2019 study found fear and stress, as well as a lack of support, especially in high poverty schools, as major contributing factors (Garcia & Weiss, p. 12). In a National

Public Radio report called "The teacher dropout crisis," Aly Seidel found that "40 to 50 percent of new teachers leave within their first five years on the job" (Seidel, 2014, para. 6).

Feelings of being unprepared and lacking support may explain why teachers often put on the best "dog and pony" show they can when an administrator is in the room, and why many teachers promise their students rewards for good behavior during an observation. Who can blame them, when they lack the skills, do not feel supported, and their evaluation scores often directly impact their abilities to keep their jobs? How do teachers create safe classrooms for students when they do not feel safe themselves?

Incidents like the one at Columbine are seared into the educational psyche. In April 2018, a Pew Research survey reported that a majority of teens say they are somewhat or very worried about the possibility of a school shooting happening at their school, and their parents share that concern (as cited in Graf, 2018, para. 1). The study reports, "Overall 57% of teens say they are worried about the possibility of a shooting happening at their school, with one-in-four saying they are very worried" (as cited in Graf, 2018, para. 4). Research suggests that violence against teachers may be rising, too. In a 2018 article, Terence Jeffrey investigated attacks on teachers by students in public schools. From a 2015–2016 report published jointly by the National Center for Education Statistics and the Bureau of Justice Statistics, Jeffrey (2019) concludes that in the 2015–2016 school year

> there was no measurable difference between the percentages of male and female public school teachers who reported being threatened with injury by a student (10 percent each). However, a higher percentage of female public school teachers reported being physically attacked (6 percent vs. 4 percent). (para. 11)

Educational leaders must accept that students and teachers can and often do *feel* unsafe at school. One way to address the flood of fears students bring to school is to help teachers develop the skills they need to create inclusive harmonious classrooms. The best way to do this is to make sure teachers feel valued and safe too.

In the book, *Flip the system: Changing education from the ground up*, Jalmer Evers and Rene Kneyber (2016) explain the problem with how the educational system views teachers today:

> In the neoliberal perspective, the teacher is viewed as a trained monkey, and it is simply a question of finding the right stick to beat him with, or the right brand of peanuts, to make him do the desired dance in front of the audience. The teacher is no longer viewed as a professional, but as a laborer who simply has to follow evidence-based methods in order to secure externally determined goals. (p. 4)

This view leaves teachers feeling unheard and resentful, caught between the needs of the students in their classrooms and the demands of the administrators who are evaluating them.

To solve this problem, the educational system should strive to create schools where teachers' voices are valued. When teachers are engaged in school's decision-making and when they collaborate with administrators at all levels they feel valued, they enjoy their job more, learning outcomes and student achievements increase, and overall school climate improves. Looking at data from the Department of Education's National Center for Education Statistics Schools and Staffing Survey, Richard Ingersoll concluded:

> Schools in which teachers have more control over key schoolwide and classroom decisions have fewer problems with student misbehavior, show more collegiality and cooperation among teachers and administrators, have a more committed and engaged teaching staff, and do a better job of retaining their teachers. (as cited in Kahlenberg & Potter, 2014, para. 4)

When teachers feel their opinions and voices are valued in decision-making they

> are 3 times more likely to encourage students to be leaders and decision makers in the classroom. . . . 4 times more likely to be excited about their future career in education. . . . [and] 4 times more likely to believe their can make a difference. (Quaglia, 2016, pp. 6–7)

In a world where violence has seeped into classrooms and where both teachers and students report feeling fearful, the key is to listen to the experts. Teachers are the ones on the ground, in the trenches, they have the firsthand knowledge. Value teachers' opinions and they are more likely to value and listen to students. Value teachers' voices and they will create classrooms where students feel valued, where students feel safe to engage in learning.

ALL DEFINITIONS OF SUCCESS MUST BE VALUED

GPA, class rank, IQ, ACT, and/or SAT scores are all valued measurement tools, frequently seen as predicators for a student's future success in life. And, while high achievement on these cognitive measurements can be linked with acceptance into college, their importance has declined in today's workplace. Research from Harvard professor, David Deming (2017), reveals that today's employees must have social or soft skills, such as teamwork and communication to be most successful (para. 2). "Workers with high social skills earn higher wages because they can specialize in the most productive tasks and trade their output with others" (Deming, 2017, para. 11).

In 1990, the U.S. government issued *The secretary's commission on achieving necessary skills*. The goal was to identify and describe the skills required for success in work. The concern was that schools were not effectively preparing students for careers. The report did not find that in order to be successful at work, students need to get more A's or do better on the SAT test. Instead, the report found that schools focused too much on skills that make good students and not enough on teaching skills that would be useful outside of the educational system—such as flexibility, problem-solving, ability to self-regulate time, ability to multitask, or the ability to work with a diverse group of people (Kane et al., 1990).

The authors explain:

> It is now becoming widely recognized that the United States must choose between two futures. We can become increasingly divided into rich and poor, a nation of second-rate products and services; or, we can continue to be a highly productive and thriving economic force. To remain the latter we must restructure our schools and workplaces and greatly increase the skills of much of our current and future workforce—especially those of our frontline, non-college educated workers. (pp. 2–3)

What this report found is intuitively known by many people but has yet to be integrated well into the educational systems. Success cannot and should not be narrowly defined by how well a student does in school. The educational system must broaden its understanding of what success looks like and must create educational environments where we prepare students for different, but equally valuable, types of success.

How?

Personalization.

According to a 2017 survey from Epsilon, a leader in branding research, "80% of respondents indicated they were more likely to do business with a company if it offered personalized experiences" (as cited in Epsilon, 2018, para. 2). If Netflix can personalize movie choices, and Nike lets customers personalize shoes, the educational system should find a way to personalize success.

One group that is trying to understand how to personalize learning is The Dark Horse Project. By examining personal stories through an ongoing long-term study, the Laboratory for the Science of Individuality at the Harvard Graduate School of Education is reframing the question of success. Instead of asking, "What is the best way to achieve success?" they are asking, "What is the best way for *you* to achieve success?" The Dark Horse Project (Rose &

Ogas, 2018) asserts that in order to help students answer this question, the education system must change the goal of education—it must be made personal.

What would happen if the educational system stopped caring about a predictable, idealized concept of success and instead worked with each child to create individualized success plans based on a student's own unique personality, goals, talents, interests, and experiences? What if the goal of education was to look for each child's "unique potential for excellence" (Rose & Ogas, 2018, p. 202)? What if Individual Education Plans were the norm for every student?

The key would be to change what outcomes are valued. One place to start could be redefining how schools assess students. Too many educators focus on deficits. They identify gaps in learning, create remediation plans to make up for lessons missed, and base forward movement in a class on a sequential understanding of learning. But, that is only one way of thinking about an individual's capacity. Programs like StrengthsFinder operate on the premise that people will do better when they understand what their talents are and not their limitations (Rath, 2007). Instead of giving students standardized tests to see what they are missing, and then try to adjust teaching or offer supplemental learning in weak areas, educators could give each student a StrengthsFinder's test and then use a student's individual strengths as a catalyst for learning.

Let me tell you a personal story to illustrate this point. In 2008, I was a young reporter, author, and mother, working for a medium-sized, but well-respected rural newspaper in New Hampshire. I had been working there for about five years and had just finished my Master of Fine Arts degree in creative non-fiction. Outside of work I had recently been finding success getting my creative pieces published in journals and magazines. One day I decided to apply for a residency at the MacDowell Colony. The residency included housing and food, and if I needed to I could even have applied for additional financial aid to cover travel or lost income.

I knew my chances of getting into the colony were slim. Approximately 2,000 artists apply each year from around the world, and on average, one in every ten was offered a residency. In fact, in 2008, the year I applied, the MacDowell Colony had roughly the same acceptance rate as most Ivy League schools. I applied anyway.

No one thought I would get in. Not just because the MacDowell was hard for everyone to get into but more specifically because I was young, twenty-eight years old, I had a five-year-old at home, and as a writer I struggled with spelling and grammar. Sure, I could write a good story, but according to the seasoned reporters around me, I was not a real writer. I did not pay enough attention to the details of how language worked. In fact, the editors at the newspaper actually kept a list of "Amanda-isms" tacked to a wall.

Every so often when they needed a good chuckle, they would pull it down and read the list. Like the time I wrote a story about a local organization designed to help blind people who "tortured" their blind peers, instead of "tutoring" them. Luckily for me the editors always caught the errors. But there was no way someone who made mistakes like I did could be accepted into such a prestigious artists' colony.

Except you know what? I was.

One of my coworkers, flummoxed by my acceptance said, "You know you got in because unlike the rest of us you're not afraid to just throw your name in and apply." Initially this statement hurt my feelings, as it was clearly meant to diminish my success and make it plausible. Ultimately, I had a wonderful time at the MacDowell Colony and decided that I had learned a lesson about envy and letting go of other peoples' perspectives.

Reflecting on the experience, I think the lesson is a little different. Maybe that older jaded reporter was correct. What made me successful was not my spelling or grammatical talent. Instead, I was successful because I possessed an ability that was not traditionally equated with the skills needed to be a good writer. What I had was the ability to try anyway.

The educational system must be transformed so that success is not defined by weakness or deficit. Just because a child struggles with spelling and grammar does not mean that student will be a bad writer. Instead, the system must value the whole child and thus ask more predictive questions such as: How much does this child read? Do they write in their spare time? Do they want to be a writer? Do they have the skills necessary to find a good editor?

The tragedy today is that the school system does not have well developed ways to teach, build, or assess these complex skills. The educational system has been built to rely on simple metrics like how well a student performs on spelling or grammar test to measure whether a student shows promise in a given area. The system has failed to value a student's ability to find and utilize supports—like an editor.

Education is not alone in needing to shift what it assesses to better fit what the world currently values. In a 2019 TED Talk, the First Minister of Scotland, Niocla Sturgeon, shared her perspective that gross domestic product should not be the measurement of a country's success. She said:

> When we focus on wellbeing, we start a conversation that provokes profound and fundamental questions. What really matters to us in our lives? What do we value in the communities we live in? What kind of country, what kind of society do we really want to be? And when we engage people in those questions, in finding the answers to those questions, then I believe that we have a much better chance of addressing the alienation and disaffection from politics that is so prevalent in so many countries across the developed world today. (para. 6)

To make this shift the First Minister worked with the governments of Iceland and New Zealand to establish the Wellbeing Economy Governments Group (WEGG). Instead of assessing success based on the amount a country produces, which may have positive short-term impacts on an economy but could then have negative long-term problems, the WEGG has placed value on measuring other things.

If countries can make this shift, then the education system can too. It starts by measuring and valuing all the skills each individual student possesses. It means educators will need to find ways to assess and encourage complex skills like communication, thoughtfulness, tenacity, and integrity—skills that help a student be successful outside of school. It starts by valuing what a student is good at and then helping them capitalize on those inherent abilities. It starts by asking what success looks like for each individual student.

THE INSIDE PERSPECTIVE MUST BE VALUED

School systems, especially large urban systems, are cumbersome, tedious, and difficult places to make change. At times, strong unions and leadership do not trust each other. A lack of shared planning and collaboration time can leave teachers feeling like isolated kings or queens in their own classrooms. Parents may have negative feelings toward school based on their own experiences and become uncooperative. Personalities, assumptions, private goals, and territories can get in the way of decision-making. In an environment where there is never enough money, teachers, or time, even the strongest agents of change can begin to feel disheartened.

The saying goes like this, "Educators believe two things: The system is broken, and change is not the answer." Social Theory from Mark Granovetter (as cited in Gladwell, 2016) called, "The Threshold Model of Collective Behavior" helps explain at least part of the reason why, despite acknowledging that things are not working as well as they could, the world of education has remained relatively unchanged. The theory asserts that behaviors will change when an individual's threshold of social pressure is reached. That threshold is unique for each person but generally represents the number of people who have to be doing something before the individual will engage in it as well.

Think about it like this. What does everyone say when they are pulled over for speeding. "Everyone else is doing it too." People know speeding is wrong, but they do it anyway because those around them are. Malcolm Gladwell (2016) in his podcast, Revisionist History, summarizes it like this, "What people believe isn't going to help much if you want to understand why they try or don't try difficult, or problematic, or strange things. You have to understand the social context in which they're operating" (para. 77). In the case of speeding the threshold of social pressure is low, it takes very few speeding cars for a person to ignore their beliefs and zoom into the fast lane. If asked later whether they believe speeding is wrong that same person may answer, "yes." Their beliefs have not changed even if how they act did.

People in education may say they want change. They may say they value personalization, or physical education, or outdoor play, or art, or competency-based grading, but when their beliefs push against what everyone else is doing, their actions will comply with the majority, and they decide to just go with the flow. This theory explains why well-meaning educators, with strong beliefs, acquiesce. No one else is standing with them. Their social threshold has not been reached, so they shrug their shoulders, throw up their hands, complain to their friends, and continue operating in whatever way the majority is.

Of course there are exceptions. There are schools, even states, that are doing education differently. What these exemplars have in common is support from the top. To move the needle, legislators must value educators and educators must value legislation. When these two groups collaborate, things happen because (1) educators know the system and (2) they are the ones who will implement it. Successful legislation, legislation that creates real change, values educators because they are the ones who will be deploying the change and because they are the ones who can anticipate the problems.

Just think of the rabbits.

Macquarie Island is the sole breeding ground for the Royal Penguin. Rabbits were not a native species, but over time they had been introduced to the island and began to take over. Concerned citizens worried that the rabbits were eating all the vegetation that the penguins needed to make their nests. So, they introduced a disease to kill the rabbits. The disease worked and most of the rabbits on the island died. This left the penguins with more vegetation for their nests. But, it also left the local feral cats no food to eat.

The cats had been eating the rabbits. Hungry, the cats started to eat the Royal Penguin chicks. So, of course, the town adopted a new program and killed off nearly all of the cats. Except, now with most of the cats gone, the rabbit population spiked again. "Since the eradication of cats eight years ago there are now an estimated 100,000 rabbits munching foliage on Macquarie Island" (Strickland, 2009, para. 4).

There are so many stories like this. Stories about trying to solve a problem and ultimately making it worse because of a lack of understanding. Today, it is undeniable that the educational system is designed to make students good at school and to get as many students as possible enrolled in college, but unfortunately we have not seen major changes in outcomes.

> Forty years of reform, accompanied by a doubling of per pupil spending, has failed to improve this picture. Standardized test scores have not budged. SAT scores have declined. More students enrolled in college, but the share of 25-year-olds with a bachelor's degree did not increase from 1995 to 2015, and it stands barely above the 1975 level. (Cass, 2018, para. 8)

If education is the key to a prosperous society, the American people have a real problem. The answer is not to reinvent the wheel by creating more charter schools. That model has been proven not to work any better. The answer is to look at the exemplars—what is working in education—and place a value on learning from these organizations. The answer is to learn from those individuals or schools who are doing education right. Learn from the people on the inside.

CONCLUSIONS

It is time to transform education, and CTE can help. CTE is a form of education that is working. It is supported by both parties, Republican and Democrat, and it provides a pathway to both career success and college.

A 2019 study from *Education Next* found that high school students who took CTE courses achieved the same college success as those students who did not (Kreisman & Stange, 2019). And, a report from the U.S. Department of Education, found that "eight years after their expected graduation date, students who focused on (CTE) courses while in high school had higher median annual earnings than students who did not focus on CTE" (U.S. Department of Education, 2019, p. 1).

According to Mike Rowe, former host of the TV show "Dirtiest Jobs," there are more than 7 million job openings waiting to be filled in fields that for the most part do not require a bachelor's degree, and "there are not enough qualified workers to fill them" (as cited in Connley, 2018, para. 2). Companies are crying out for employees, and they are turning to creative partnerships with education to solve the problem.

For example, Walmart and Lowes have both partnered with a company called Guild to offer employees nearly free college courses and even college planning while working. Starbucks, McDonalds, and Chipotle Mexican Grill also offer reduced college tuition for their employees. Companies invest in education because they are hungry for employees, and it is a proven way to attract and retain them.

Whelen Engineering in New Hampshire measured and created a plastic injection mold to make a propeller for underwater robots. The mold cost $8,000. Whelen not only donated the mold to a local high school as a way to promote the field and reach students, but they also went to the high school and showed the students how to use it.

Electrical students are finding that electricians are paying for their apprenticeship license while they are in high school, with the understanding that they will apprentice with that company once they graduate. Automotive dealers are banding together and creating scholarships to send high school students to local two-year automotive programs.

The corrections department in a rural northern New England state is working to develop a program to teach high school students about protective services, through a partnership with the local prison. And since the school cannot afford to pay a teacher, the corrections department is willing to send in their employees to run the class.

An officer of corrections only needs a high school diploma or equivalent, can start working at nineteen years of age, and earns $11 per hour more than that state's minimum wage. They also get full life insurance, hazard pay, dental and medical insurance, and a pension. For many students this would also be a viable and affordable pathway toward becoming a police officer, without the debt accrued through earning a four-year criminal justice degree.

Now is the time.

Now is the time for America to shrug off the stigma around vocational education and purposefully develop links between the trades, certification programs, colleges, and business leaders. The education system needs to focus on showing students and families that there are options to move fluidly from employment to education and back again. Schools must integrate job training and work-based experiences into the school day in meaningful ways, and then encourage companies to cooperate with the development of these programs.

It is time for educators to embrace new approaches and collaborations because businesses and legislators cannot be left to reimagining solutions without the input of educators. For example, New Hampshire legislators created a bill that required the creation of a board to set the vision for CTE across the state. Board members include CTE directors, superintendents, business representatives, and legislators.

This group recently worked with the house and senate to support giving tax credits to businesses that donate equipment, materials, and/or time to any CTE program. This bill is not an instant fix, but it does represent a usable, viable, and useful solution to developing more work-based programming for high school students.

The current educational system in the United States teaches and values a narrow set of skills. This must change. In part because the skills that are being fostered are not those needed for success in today's world, and in part because supporting a limited number of skills has created a value system that leaves many students out.

Education cannot be set up as a dichotomy with rigorous academics on one side and relevant engaging learning on the other. Instead, educational leaders should use CTE classes to evolve education, creating classes that are both rigorous and relevant. Businesses and legislators must listen to and work with educational insiders, to develop a new vision for what the role of education is, and how it will be measured.

This new vision must be based on individual student's assets and passions and must be personally tailored to meet each student's specific needs and drives. And, the word that must reverberate continuously in the minds of those who seek to shift the system must be: value. All students, teachers' voices, career pathways, and skills must be seen as critical. It is not enough to say that the education system is working for many. The new goal for education must be based on valuing individual success for every child. Every. Single. One.

Chapter 5

Challenging *Status Quo* From One Superintendent's Perspective

Ruthann Petruno-Goguen

Superintendents are faced with making important decisions the minute they accept the job as School Superintendent. The most important decision superintendents need to make is whether they are willing to lead, implement, and follow through with action plans that will challenge *status quo*. For clarity, *status quo* is anything that interferes with ensuring *all* students are provided equitable access to optimal learning environments in which to discover their individual talents.

Superintendents need to make a conscious decision: Are they going to *go along to get along* by keeping the adult population happy by not asking them to do anything differently? Or, are they going to push through the resistance that emerges when organizational systems are challenged and lead the change that is necessary to ensure educators are updating instructional strategies to meet the diverse learning needs of today's students?

Unfortunately, many public education systems and structures are not designed to meet the diverse learning needs of all students. Ask any high school student who you might know the following questions:

- How are you engaged in your learning?
- How often are you able to share your independent thoughts as they relate to what you are learning in your classrooms?
- How is the context of what you are learning connected to your everyday life? To your future?
- How often are you involved in collaborative group work in your classrooms?
- How often are you asked to solve problems and explain your strategies?
- What type of choices do you have in your classrooms to demonstrate what you know and are able to do?

- What type of hands-on and multisensory learning experiences do you have?
- What is the best part of your learning experience?

The answers to these questions will most likely inform you that the typical classroom has not changed much over the past hundred years. Teachers teach, and students listen with one mission—to regurgitate information and pass a test. Conformity permeates most school classrooms and hallways, and far too many students are taught to be dependent learners rather than independent thinkers in public schools (Hammond, 2015).

Robinson (2017) informs us that many young people "have lost all hope of being able to work for a decent living," and they are "vulnerable to underemployment and poverty" (p. 58). Ironically, public education was founded on the ideal that education was a way to ensure freedom for all, yet it is the breeding ground where different rules and opportunities are granted to people based on their socioeconomic class or ability to pass a standardized test.

Status quo is interfering with ensuring all students are cared for and provided high-quality learning opportunities in which to discover their individual talents and passions. There is a tremendous amount of pressure on educators, especially superintendents, to set the dial tone and rate of speed for which *status quo* is challenged in school organizations, because far too many students are not discovering their fullest potential.

This chapter takes a closer look at the dangers of maintaining *status quo* cultures in school systems. It discusses, conformity in public education, the importance of maintaining a democratic society, the dangers of high-stakes testing and labels, technology and the brain, cultural biases, reading data, tenure and entitlement, and research-based evidence to support the need for public education systems to change. Most importantly, this chapter connects the mindsets of educators to school culture and links these two factors to how well any school is able to make effective progress with meeting the diverse needs of all our students.

The following assumptions guides this superintendent's perspective:

- Every student must be valued and respected.
- Success looks differently for each student and teacher.
- Improving student success rates requires educators to reflect upon their spoken and unspoken core values.
- Educators must be willing to modify their day-to-day practices and intentional instructional strategies.
- Education must be transformed from the inside out in order for it to be effective and sustainable.

SAVING A DEMOCRATIC SOCIETY THROUGH PUBLIC EDUCATION

Public education is the one gateway available to everyone in America to ensure that a democratic society exists. Public education is credited for providing all people (regardless of their economic status, race, gender, etc.) relevant learning opportunities with the ultimate goal of having all individuals discover their own talents and passions. Once discovered, these talents and passions are the foundations for *how* individuals eventually develop into contributing members of our democratic and global society.

Public education systems are held responsible to protect and ensure all students have equal rights to a free and appropriate education. The federal government, states, and local communities all have systems of accountability, where they measure success by student achievement testing results. Data trends in public education indicate particular subgroups of learners (e.g., the economically disadvantaged, second language learners, special education, and high-risk students) are not making adequate progress.

The question is, *Why are some groups of students not finding success in our public schools?* The answer begins with *It is not the student's fault*. The act of educating one's self is a basic right and not a privilege in the United States. Education itself represents freedom—the freedom to change one's economic status, the freedom to develop one's individual belief system, and the freedom to discover one's unlimited potential as a human being.

Data trends indicate we have a great divide between those who can achieve on the standardized tests and those who cannot. There will be lasting negative effects on the development of our democratic society if we do not take action to address the social injustices that are happening in our public schools today.

Labeling Students

We know the current model of public education is far from perfect. It places top-performing students in high-level classes, it assists the students who are struggling with remedial or intervention programming, and it ignores students who end up being classified as the middle of the road learners. Why do the top-performing students inherently get trusted more, given more freedom to express their creativity, and exposed to more problem-solving and performance tasks? Why do middle- and low-performing students get restricted to certain types of classes, where the rigor is lower and often associated with rote memory tasks?

The labels that educators place upon students are really imposed judgments about their capabilities. These labels and the environments that are then created to support these labels, send students implicit and explicit messages on what they are capable of doing. Students eventually believe what they are being told by the adults in their lives. Labels can be damaging and can impact a student's engagement level with discovering their own talents and passions.

If public education is the breeding ground to ensure a democratic society, we need to examine why certain groups of students are falling behind, labeled, and not provided equitable opportunities for discovering their truest and fullest potential. Is it not best practice to continue with the *status quo* of having educators label a student's potential at a young age and having that label follow them through their K-12 journey?

Conformity Is Not Working for All Students

We have a "one size fits all" model in most public schools, and only the students who fit into the conformity and compliance structures, which have traditionally defined our public school systems, are the ones who find success. The public education model has not changed since the Industrial Revolution. In the simplest terms, teachers teach and students comply by sitting down, listening, and regurgitating curriculum content in a prescribed fashion to pass a test. Everyone knows the students who are able to follow the rules are the ones who are deemed successful by educators.

Diversity is not taken into consideration in public education and not all students have equitable opportunities to discover their individual talents because *status quo* prevails in public education. Students, teachers, and administrators, alike, are all conforming to ancient rules of public education—the bell rings, it's English . . . the bell rings, it's mathematics . . . the bell rings, it's science . . . the bell rings, it's art . . . the bell rings, it's lunch time . . . the bell rings, the day is over, only to start again tomorrow with the same repetitive pattern.

This traditional model of schooling prioritizes academic subjects, puts less value on the arts, and rarely takes an interdisciplinary approach to teaching. Conforming to *status quo* structures of yesteryear is particularly difficult for many students, especially those who are living in poverty.

Students living in poverty come to school with different needs and skills, and Payne (2005) points out that most educators do not have the lens or real-life exposures to poverty to understand how to create school environments that counteract the limitations poverty has on learning. Jensen (2009) reminds us, "If we want students to change, we must change ourselves and the environments students spend time in every day" (p. 48). This is the real challenge—the adults in public education need to change first in order to meet the diverse needs of the students who sit before them each day.

TODAY'S STUDENTS ARE DIFFERENT BECAUSE OF TECHNOLOGY

Through the advances of technology, today's students obtain and process information very differently than their teachers and parents did when they were in school, yet the classroom structure has changed little over the years. Today's students have been growing up in a fast-paced digital world, where literally any type of information is a "swipe" away and at their fingertips.

Technology puts students' in the driver's seat. They no longer have to wait for a teacher to provide information, all they have to do is ask Siri, Alexa, or Google, to find out the answer to any question they may have. Yet with all these advances in technology *status quo* prevails in public education and today's classrooms are structured in ways where the teacher stands and delivers for fifty to ninety minutes and the students continue to be passive participants.

Today's students' brains are very used to switching tasks and quickly scanning information on their digital devices. This type of processing only requires surface-level thinking where tons of information goes in and out of the short-term memory (Sousa, 2016). While today's students may actually be addicted to the constant interruptions of switching tasks on their digital devices, it is important to note "a person who is interrupted during a task, may take up to 50% longer to finish the task and make up to 50% more errors" (Medina, 2008, as cited in Sousa, 2017, p. 32).

So, the question for educators is, *How do we create new environments in today's classrooms that balance maintaining students' interest levels, with purposeful interruptions linked to deep learning?* The National Governors Association's study (2005) surveyed over 10,500 high school students and found that "more than one third of the students said their school had not done a good job challenging them to think critically and analyze problems," and they were thinking about dropping out because they were "not learning anything" (as citied in Sousa, 2017, p. 34).

With "only a little more than half of high school graduates able to meet the demands of first-year college level reading, based on a national readiness indicator" (ACT Report, 2006, as cited in Sousa, 2017, p. 33), the time has come to challenge the *status quo* in public education.

Fixed Mindsets

The current model of public education fails to see "every child is, by nature a unique individual with innate talents and sensibilities" (Robinson, 2017, p. 152) and these failures are connected to the "fixed mindset" (Dweck, 2016) of the adults who work in and run schools and districts. Most adults in public education believe the traditional model of schooling that they experienced was good enough for them, so it should be good enough for today's students. The problem with this fixed mindset is that it ignores the fact that today's students think and retain information in markedly different ways than their teachers, because they have grown up in a technological world (Sousa, 2016).

The public education system is broken because it is rigid and inflexible. It does not celebrate and respect individual differences or respect diverse thinking. Robinson (2017) reminds us the current model of education is its own worst enemy:

> We ask how we can raise academic standards but not whether they will provide what we need to survive the future. We ask where we can find talented people but ignore the talents of people that surround us. We look but we do not see, because our traditional common-sense assessment of abilities distracts us from what is actually there. We ask how to promote creativity and innovation but stifle the processes and conditions that are most likely to bring them about. Caught in an old worldview, we continue to lean on the twin pillars of mass education, despite the evidence that the system is faltering for so many people within it. (p. 89)

Summary

The truth is public education is not consistently ensuring equitable and diverse opportunities exist for *all* learners to find success in school, and this endangers the future of our democratic society. Public education is not consistently reinforcing a constructivist approach where *all* students can create their own meaning from what they are learning. It is not providing *all* students various opportunities to discover their own strengths as critical thinkers. It is not ensuring *all* students are provided the necessary interventions to learn how to read and comprehend an assortment of texts at proficient levels.

We have students requiring a quick-paced technologically driven classroom environment where they have choice and voice. However, we have teachers who are accustomed to leading the learning and maintaining a conformity model in their classrooms.

HOW ARE WE VALUING EVERY STUDENT IN PUBLIC EDUCATION?

The answer is, by their testing results. Herein lies the problem, one test, or a series of standardized tests, does not accurately measure one human being's worth or potential to learn, think, or contribute to a global society. Many politicians and educators would argue this point simply because millions of dollars have been spent creating an ever-changing accountability system that rates, measures, ranks, and classifies not only students but also teachers, administrators, and superintendents on their abilities to change test scores.

The assumption is that "a test" is the only valid and reliable way to view how students have created meaning from what they are learning. While an accountability system is needed to measure what is being taught to students, schools need to incorporate multiple measures of authentic assessments that allow students to show what they know and are able to do.

The Remediation Cycle

As mentioned, labels are dangerous, and too often socioeconomic status, test scores, and grades become the easy ways to label and classify students into particular groups. We know, the students who can answer questions quickly are labeled as high achievers, and the students who need a differentiated learning environment or more supports are labeled as struggling learners.

Unfortunately, the struggling learner is often put into classes where the rigor is less, simply because the adults have decided the struggling student cannot handle deep learning or high-level rigorous content. When in fact the struggling learner may simply need more time, more hands-on and kinesthetic approaches, or more visual components incorporated in their learning environment.

If teachers take a closer look at their own schools or any low-performing school, they may find that there are large numbers of students who are one to two grade level behind in the basic skill of reading. Teachers may also see a direct correlation between a student's socioeconomic status and their scores.

Living in poverty and chronic stress impacts a student's ability to take in and retain information (Jensen, 2009). About 40 percent of students living in chronic poverty have developed deficiencies by the age of three in at least two areas of functioning, such as language and emotional responsiveness (Jensen, 2009). All educators are responsible for fixing this social justice problem in public schools.

A common solution to fixing this problem is to increase the amount of time for explicit instruction and direct remediation strategies. When there are large groups of students not reaching reading proficiency, it becomes difficult to keep the balance between teaching grade-level content and finding the time for more remediation. Sometimes, core grade-level instruction is eventually replaced or takes a back seat to the remediation.

A Case Study

The process of having remediation replace core grade-level instruction can happen without educators really even noticing it. For example, one rural elementary school labeled and placed students into groups starting in kindergarten, based on their Dynamic Indicators of Basic Early Literacy Skills scores (University of Oregon Center on Teaching and Learning, 2018). Students were placed in the *High Achieving*, *On Target*, or *Below Target groups* and these groups seldom changed as students progressed up through the grades.

Due to the large number of students in the *Below Target group*, the teachers would focus more on remediation, and in time, these students fell further and further behind on their grade-level content, simply because it was not taught to them.

In the *Below Target group*, the teacher would rotate to meet with small groups of students to provide explicit and direct instruction and expect the rest of the class to work independently on low-level tasks, such as worksheets. As you can imagine this did not work well, because *all* the students in the *Below Target group* required ongoing supports to close their learning gaps, and working independently for the majority of the class only pushed them further behind.

The intentions of the teachers were to assist students with closing their learning gaps, but the result of not focusing on grade-level content and high standards, essentially had students falling further and further behind. The *Below Target group* suffered the most because they were only exposed to low-level, skill and drill types of tasks. Without realizing it, this practice of labeling and leveling students based on a test score created very little time for explicit grade-level instruction or the opportunities for students to move out of their predetermined group to another group.

The goal of remediation is to assist students with closing learning gaps, but all too often, the remediation itself is done in isolation and it does not explicitly connect to the grade-level learning that is happening in the classroom. When this happens, many students fall further behind, because they are unable to independently make the connection between the skills they are remediating to the content they are learning in the classroom.

Sadly, some educators are unconsciously lowering expectations for students labeled as struggling learners, and these lower expectations essentially require students to do *less*, when they actually need *more* practice with applying their skills. The typical classroom teacher assesses understanding by asking open-ended questions and once a few of the top-performing students answer correctly, the teacher typically moves on to the next topic. This model leaves students, who need more time to process and produce answers, lost in the dust. Once again, the struggling student is not expected to perform in the classroom and this pattern perpetuates a cycle of remediation.

Educators Resist Change

Even though educators constantly talk about the high numbers of students not reaching grade-level mastery, many school systems do nothing to change the fact that the number of students not meeting grade-level standards continues to grow. *Status quo* prevails in public education, because far too many adults prioritize being comfortable with their own day-to-day actions, rather than working to discover new methods of meeting the diverse needs of the students they are serving. The reality is, the majority of educators are resistant to any type of change that requires them to veer away from their day-to-day practices, so labeling students by their test scores remains a common practice.

This cycle is especially dangerous for the struggling student. Low-performing students get labeled by their test scores, tracked into a remediation pathway, receive less and less core instruction, and this pattern actually widens their learning gaps. The assumption is that struggling learners cannot produce in the traditional classroom setting, but the truth is the adults are maintaining the systems and structures that continually marginalize our students.

The adults assume students who are unable to conform to the traditional classroom practices of sitting quietly in class, answering questions when called upon, and regurgitating information on a test are the problem and have deficits. This line of thinking is dangerous.

The culture of *status quo* has such a long-standing history in public education, and this is going to be very difficult to change without a major paradigm shift in our own thinking. This shift in thinking needs to occur with the adults' mindsets and not the students' mindsets. The assumption that today's students can learn in the traditional model of schooling, because it worked for the adults, is crippling more and more learners each day. The question for educators is, *Why are educators allowing status quo to continue when they know it is not effective for all students?*

Cultural Biases

Cultural beliefs and biases also come into play when discussing how standardized tests are not an accurate reflection of what someone knows and can do. Do the test creators, the curriculum resources, or educators really understand the multiple cultures represented in our student populations? How is it even possible for the questions on any one standardized assessment to possibly take into consideration all the diverse cultures represented in our student population?

It is not. So, educators need to consider how cultural testing biases also negatively impact our students' results. Although most adults understand cultural and testing biases exist, rarely are these topics addressed in public school settings, because everyone falls back to the comfort level of their own views and *status quo* continues rather than fixing the problems that exist.

According to the National Center of Children Living in Poverty (2019), over 72 million children live in families whose annual income is below the federal poverty level. This is concerning on many levels. Poor students are treated differently than their peers (Jensen, 2009); The Massachusetts State Equity Report Update (Massachusetts Department of Elementary & Secondary Education, 2018) and most educators are not equipped to understand the significant impacts poverty has on the developing child (Payne, 2005).

Educators need to work harder at creating school environments that counteract the limitations poverty has on learning. Instead educators are committed to a high-stake testing environment, where we judge a student's potentials based on scores, even though we know the ways in which the tests were created are biased.

Some of the learning gaps that exist within some subgroups (e.g., economically disadvantaged, special education, Hispanic, second language learners) are really resource gaps that are not being properly addressed in public schools. Unfortunately, some students receive the message that they are not good enough to succeed, they give up hope, lose the desire to use their imaginations, and eventually stop trying to learn. We are diminishing the talent pool for the future, by holding on to a public education system that is failing far too many students.

Reading Scores

The National Assessment of Educational Progress (NAEP) reading scores, produced by the U. S. Department of Education, will demonstrate how testing data can be used to tell two very different stories. Tables 5.1–5.3 show the historical pattern of 20 percent to 40 percent of our students in grades 12, 8, and 4 scoring in the Below Basic category in Reading between the years of 1992 and 2017.

A review of the NAEP scores for reading (see table 5.4) indicates that females consistently score higher than males and the gap increases with time—6 points difference in grade 4 and 10 points difference in grades 8 and 12. Asian students consistently score higher than all other races/ethnicities and there is a marked difference when comparing their data to the Hispanic, Native American, and black students; for the Hispanic subgroup there is a 32, 29, and 21 point difference in grades 4, 8, and 12, respectively; for the Native American subgroup there is a 39, 31, and 18 point difference in grades 4, 8, and 12, respectively; for the black subgroup there is a 35, 35, and 31 point difference in grades 4, 8, and 12, respectively. Asian students also surpassed white students by a 9, 9, and 2 point difference in grades 4, 8, and 12, respectively.

Table 5.1 Grade 12 NAEP Reading Scores

Year	Below Basic	Basic	Proficient	Advanced
1992	20	39	36	4
1994	25	38	32	4
1998	24	36	35	6
2002	26	38	31	5
2005	27	37	31	5
2009	26	36	33	5
2013	25	37	32	5
2015	28	35	31	6

Source: The Nation's Report Card (n.d.).

Table 5.2 Grade 8 NAEP Reading Scores

Year	Below Basic	Basic	Proficient	Advanced
1992	31	40	26	3
1994	30	40	27	3
1998	27	41	30	3
2002	25	43	30	3
2003	26	42	29	3
2005	27	42	28	3
2007	26	43	28	3
2009	25	43	30	3
2011	24	42	30	3
2013	22	42	32	4
2015	24	42	31	4
2017	24	40	32	4

Source: The Nation's Report Card (n.d.).

Table 5.3 Grade 4 NAEP Reading Scores

Year	Below Basic	Basic	Proficient	Advanced
1992	38	34	22	6
1994	40	31	22	7
1998	40	30	22	7
2000	41	30	23	7
2002	36	32	24	7
2003	37	32	24	8
2005	36	33	24	8
2007	33	34	25	8
2009	33	34	25	8
2011	33	34	26	8
2013	32	33	27	8
2015	31	33	27	9
2017	32	31	27	9

Source: The Nation's Report Card (n.d.).

Table 5.4 Race/Ethnicity NAEP Reading Scores

Variable	Grade 4 (2017)	Grade 8 (2017)	Grade 12 (2015)
Female	225	272	292
Male	219	262	282
Asian	241	284	297
White	232	275	295
Two or more races	227	272	295
Hispanic	209	255	276
Pacific Islander	212	255	N/A
Native American	202	253	279
Black	206	249	266
High Poverty	205	250	266
ELL	189	226	240

Source: The Nation's Report Card (n.d.).

Notes: Grade 4: Basic—208; Proficient—238; Advanced—268 (National Center for Education Statistics, 2018).

Grade 8: Basic—243; Proficient—281; Advanced—323 (National Center for Education Statistics, 2018).

Grade 12: Basic—265; Proficient—302; Advanced—346 (National Center for Education Statistics, 2018).

Students in the High Poverty and black subgroups scored below every group, except for English Language Learner (ELL) students (grades 4, 8, and 12) and Native American students (grade 4 only). ELL student data are dramatically lower than white students with a 43, 49, and 55 point difference in grades 4, 8, and 12, respectively. ELL student data are also markedly lower than the lowest scoring subgroups of High Poverty and black students—16 points lower than High Poverty students and 17 points lower than black students in grade 4; 24 points lower than High Poverty students and 23 points lower than black students in grade 8; and 26 points lower than High Poverty and black students in grade 12.

Interpreting the Data

The educational conversations in public schools and in the political arena often focus on test scores. NAEP results are part of many politicians' speeches to demonstrate how the public education system is failing, because too many students are not reaching advance or proficient levels of achievement in reading. While I do believe reading is an essential skill, and public education needs to be transformed, it is very important to show another perspective on the interpretation of the NAEP scores.

Ravitch (2014) reminds us that "all definitions of educational standards are subjective" (p. 47), and the National Assessment Governing Board (NAGB) developed the NAEP achievement levels based on ranges not grade-level mastery. Ravitch (2014) equates advanced to an A+; proficient to an A or

B+; "basic" to a B or C; and below basic to a D (p. 47) and reminds us that it is not realistic to think all students will fall into one category, classification, or grade.

Ravitch (2014) challenges the negative narrative associated with the NAEP scores and argues the NAEP scores have in fact improved over time:

- "Reading scores in the 4th and 8th grade have improved slowly, steadily, and significantly since 1992 for almost every group of students" (p. 49–50).
- "The proportion of 4th grade students who were proficient or advanced increased from 1992 to 2001. In 1992, 29% of students were proficient or above; in 2011, it was 34%" (p. 49). In 2017, it was 36% (see table 5.3).
- "The portion of 4th grade students who were Below Basic declined from 38% in 1992 to 33% in 2011" (p. 49). In 2017, 32% of students in grade 4 were Below Basic (see table 5.3).
- "The scores of white students, black students, Hispanic students, and Asian students in 4th grade were higher in 2011 than in 1992. The only group that saw a decline was American Indian students" (p. 50).
- "The proportion of 8th grade students who were Proficient or Advanced increased from 1992 to 2001. In 1992, 29% of students were proficient or above; in 2011, it was 34%" (p. 50). For 2017, 36% of eighth grade students were Proficient or Advanced (see table 5.2).
- "The proportion of 8th grade students who were Below Basic declined from 31% in 1992 to 24% in 2011" (p. 50). In 2017, the percentage remained at 24% (see table 5.2).
- "The scores of white students, black students, Hispanic students, Asian students, and American Indian students in 8th grade were higher in 2011 than in 1992" (p. 50).

Two opposing views on the NAEP results are shared to demonstrate that *success* means something different to everyone. One group may interpret the NAEP data to be concerning, because they see little change in the reading achievement scores since 1992. Another group may claim one large-scale assessment does not accurately reflect an individual's reading progression, because all testing is subjective. Educators need to pause, reflect, and take action, to ensure testing data are not misused to limit another human being's potential.

Lack of Racial Diversity

On the surface level the NAEP data are quite alarming, because everyone knows reading is an essential skill and the gateway to understanding all other content areas. With a range between 24 percent and 32 percent of our students in grades, 4, 8, and 12 falling into the Below Basic reading category on NAEP testing, people may conclude that public education is failing, because 24 percent to 32 percent of our students are earning what would be considered close to a grade of a D or below in this Below Basic category.

Many may be wondering: *Why are educators satisfied with a model of schooling that puts certain subgroups in lesser positions than others?* Some may look closer at the data and determine black, Hispanic, ELL, and Native American subgroups have a lower-scaled reading score than the white subgroup and may come to the conclusion that discrimination is occurring.

According to *The State of Racial Diversity in the Educator Workforce Report* (U.S. Department of Education, 2016), in 2011–2012, 80 percent of public school principals were white, 10 percent were black, and 7 percent were Hispanic (p. 7); and 82 percent of public school teachers were white and only 8 percent were Hispanic (p. 6). Our teaching force does not adequately represent our student population.

The Massachusetts State Equity Plan Update (Massachusetts Department of Elementary & Secondary Education, 2018) data (see table 5.5) indicate the proportions of teachers and students by race/ethnicity: 92.3 percent of white teachers for 61.3 percent white students; 2.8 percent Hispanic teachers for 19.4 percent Hispanic students; 2.8 percent African American/black teachers for 8.0 percent African American/black students; 1.4 percent Asian teachers for 6.7 percent Asian students; 0.06 percent others for 3.7 percent other students.

Is there a connection to be made between the fact that most educators are white and the particular subgroups that are not reaching proficiency are not white? The purpose of *The Massachusetts State Equity Report Update* (Massachusetts Department of Elementary & Secondary Education, 2018) was to analyze equity gaps in schools and districts. With 40.6 percent of the districts and 42.4 percent of the schools in Massachusetts having one or more equity gaps; and 786 schools in 263 districts having one or more school-wide gaps; and 165 school districts having one or more district-wide gaps; educators need to ask the right questions to understand how to remedy equity gaps.

The Massachusetts State Equity Report Update (Massachusetts Department of Elementary & Secondary Education, 2018) looked closely at how

Table 5.5 2016–2017 Massachusetts Data on Race/Ethnicity of Teachers and Students

Groups	White	Hispanic	African American/Black	Asian	Other
Teachers (%)	92.3	2.8	2.8	1.4	0.6
Students (%)	61.3	19.4	8.0	6.7	3.7

Source: Massachusetts Department of Elementary & Secondary Education (2018).

often low-performing subgroups had access to highly qualified teachers and discovered:

- Students of color are 79% more likely than white students to be assigned to a teacher rated Needs Improvement or Unsatisfactory (p. 1).
- Hispanic or Latino students are more than two times as likely as white students to be assigned to a teacher with low evaluation ratings (p. 1).
- Economically disadvantaged students are 75% more likely to be assigned to a teacher rated Needs Improvement or Unsatisfactory (p. 1).
- English Language Learners are 73% more likely to be assigned to a teacher rated Needs Improvement or Unsatisfactory (p. 1).

Summary

All educational conversations either start or end with the test results. The accountability system is designed to classify students into levels. The test score sets the level of expectations placed on each student. The level of expectations then creates a predetermined path for each student. Classifications begin with the test score and if students have low-test scores, they receive messages that they have failed to succeed.

Unfortunately for our students, the way in which we use test results has blurred the true purpose of what public education was designed to do, and that is, to inspire all students to reach their highest potential.

THE *STATUS QUO*

Status quo prevails in public education, and educators continue to ignore the damage being done by judging and tracking students by their test scores. Too often, teachers continue to dismiss how cultural biases can negatively impact learning environments. In too many schools, teachers continue to treat students differently because of their economic status, race, or color (Massachusetts Department of Elementary & Secondary Education, 2018).

Today's public education systems too often:

- prioritize adult's needs and egos before students' social, emotional, and academic needs;
- focus on testing results rather than learning processes, metacognition, emotional safety, cultural differences, and creativity;
- do not readily implement multisensory approaches to learning; and
- do not use multiple measures or authentic types of assessments to guide students to the next level in their personal development.

Student Success Is Not the Priority

Although educators talk about their passionate attempts to help all students learn, the reality is, there are several conflicting definitions between the ways teachers, students, and administrators define what success looks like in public education. Some teachers may define success based on how much work they actually have to do each day to prepare for their classes, or the number of A's they give out for grades, or how much money they are making.

Some students may define success based on the number of A's they receive for grades, or how they feel about coming to school each day, or whether they feel safe and valued by their teachers and peers. Some administrators may define success based on the number of students passing statewide assessments, or the number of students going to college, or the number of complaints they have to deal with each day, or the amount of money they make.

Much like the definition of *success*, the definition of *success for students* is different depending on whom you ask. Some teachers may define *success for students* based on test scores, or how easy or difficult it is to work with their students. Some students may define success based on how stressful or stress-free schools are, or how successful their social lives are in school, or on the number of As they receive for grades.

Some administrators may define *success for students* based on graduation rates, the number of students on the honor roll, or the percentage of students who enroll in college. As one can see, there are many perspectives to be found inside a public school organization, and with varying perspectives comes the opportunity for divisions.

Divisions can result from the unconscious and conscious biases of educators. Divisions can develop because different subgroups of students are treated differently. Divisions can evolve as a result of the power imbalances that exist between teachers and students and administrators and teachers. Public school organizations are living organisms, with many competing moving parts, and, unfortunately, student success is not the primary focus for everyone working in a public school organization.

The same pattern of resistance exists in public school organizations, regardless of location. Whether it is a rural, suburban, or urban school district, the people who stand up and advocate for putting students' needs first are often criticized for pointing out how the system is not working for a particular student or group of students. People who work in public education are most likely very familiar with what happens to educators who muster up the courage to challenge the way a particular student or group of students are being treated unfairly as a result of the established structures.

Educators who push against the system are often criticized, labeled, and sometimes ostracized by those who value *status quo*. Advocating for change on behalf of the children can be a thankless job. But continuing to accept a public school system that ignores that some of our children are being left behind because of their socioeconomic status or testing scores is a serious threat to the future of our democratic society.

READING AND CRITICAL-THINKING SKILLS ARE NOT BEING DEVELOPED

Our future is dependent upon having diverse and creative thinkers, yet we have public school structures that revolve around conformity and compliance. This model of conformity limits far too many students from developing their reading skills and using their critical-thinking skills. In most schools, the top-performing students are usually the only ones that are trusted to use their voices and critical-thinking skills on a day-to-day basis.

As we have seen, the NAEP (see tables 5.1–5.4) data support questioning the effectiveness of how schools are teaching reading skills. With particular subgroups falling dramatically behind other subgroups, educators need to reassess what is going on in the typical classroom. According to Sousa (2017), high school students claim, "their school had not done a good job challenging them to think critically and analyze problems" (p. 34). Teachers need to figure out new methods to ensure *all* students are learning how to become contributing members of a global society.

Developing Independent Thinkers the Montessori Way

If students were given more opportunities to be heard, they would be able to share their own creative ideas about their learning process. *Then* teachers could use that information to enhance their lessons and classroom environment. Too many teachers continue to treat students as dependent thinkers rather than independent thinkers, and this is not working for students and it is detrimental to society. When students are given opportunities to provide meaningful feedback to their teachers regarding the content of what they are learning, the nature of this type of engagement process reinforces them to become more independent thinkers.

Educators need to challenge the current model of conformity and create learning environments where *all* students' voices, thoughts, and feelings, are valued as the key components of any lesson. Students need to act as *explorers* every day in every class. All students in Montessori schools are provided the necessary *time* they need to connect to, create, and build upon, what they are learning. This is markedly different than what occurs in a traditional public school classroom where the teacher moves on after ensuring *some* students understand the concepts being taught.

The Montessori philosophy is grounded in the belief that students must own the responsibility for their own learning process, and teachers are there to serve as guides. The Montessori classroom is multi-aged and students learn from each other and by doing things independently and in groups. All learning is self-directed and self-paced in a Montessori classroom, and students act as critical thinkers, explorers, and scientists every minute of every day. A passion for discovering new knowledge is instilled in all learners, and learning is defined as an exploratory process where mistakes are welcomed.

In Montessori schools, all students develop a particular level of grit and stamina (Duckworth, 2016) because they are taught that failing at something is part of the learning process and nothing to be ashamed about. In traditional public schools, teachers may be inadvertently limiting the ways in which students can become critical thinkers by sticking to a model that is based on conformity. In traditional public schools, students are often made to feel embarrassed when they give the wrong answer, and students who get the right answer are the ones the teacher praises.

Haves and Have-Nots

Our current educational model perpetuates a cycle of marginalizing certain subgroups for one reason or another. If schools continue to keep this current model of public education, they are contributing to the creation of a social division that separates people based on their testing results, economic status, and/or race. Public education is inadvertently creating a divide in our society by adhering to the *status quo* that continues to label students into groups (e.g., college-bound, special needs, struggling students).

These labels divide people into *haves* and *have-nots*. The divide between the *haves* and the *have-nots* is further complicated by Kai-Fu Lee's (2018) claims that technology has the potential for artificial intelligence to replace both the physical and the mental workloads of humans. Knowing that public schools continue to struggle with teaching basic reading skills to all students (see tables 5.1–5.4), the thought of how easy it may become for artificial intelligence to replace the human thought process is quite frightening.

Is it possible that humans will become so reliant on technology for any new knowledge that reading skills may become a thing of the past? Lee's (2018) statements that schools are preparing students for a future that people know nothing about give us good reason to pause and reflect upon the necessity of changing the current model of public education. Schools must ensure all students become independent thinkers, fluid readers, and critical thinkers.

If some teachers are not preparing students to read and think, how will they compete with artificial intelligence in the future?

Robinson (2017) reminds us that 30 percent of current ninth-grade students in the United States will not graduate from high school, and these rates are higher when looking specifically at Native American communities where this increases to 50 percent (p. 57). With approximately 75 million young people between the ages of fifteen and twenty-four unemployed (Robinson, 2017, p. 58), one could surmise that the public education system is failing to meet the old fashioned American definition of what success is—*to be able to get a job and support oneself.*

The reality is public school systems are creating societal divides by race, color, economic status, and gender, and large groups of young people "have lost all hope of being able to work for a decent living" and are "vulnerable to underemployment and poverty" (Robinson, 2017, p. 58). The ironic part of this is that public education was founded on the ideal that education was a way to ensure freedoms for all.

Thomas Jefferson wrote to James Warren in 1179:

> If Virtue & Knowledge are diffused among the People, they will never be enslaved. This will be their great Security. Virtue & Knowledge will forever be an even Balance for Powers & Riches. I hope our Countrymen will never depart from the Principles & Maxims which have been handed down to us from our wise forefathers. This greatly depends upon the Example of Men of Character & Influence of the present Day. This is a Subject my Heart is much set upon. (Cushing, 1904, pp. 123–24)

A Failing System

Given the ideal of education is not being fulfilled for *all* students, how much longer will educators, politicians, and legislators continue to stand on the platform that public education is working to ensure the freedoms for *all*? How long will it take for the majority of students to be classified as *not proficient* under the current model? Robinson (2017) reminds us: "All organizations are perishable. They are created by people and need to be constantly revitalized if they are to survive" (p. 10). Why do we continue to resist making changes in public education that will ensure *all* students are actively learning?

We spend approximately $29,000 to incarcerate one person, and we spend approximately $9,000 on a typical high school student's education (Robinson, 2017, p. 60). These figures tell a true story; the survival of the public education system is really not a priority for our society. If our society prioritized education, we would be looking closer at the connection between appropriately funding public schools and leveling the playing field so all students have equitable access to develop into high functioning global citizens. We would be more focused on closing resource gaps in communities that have numbers of economically disadvantaged students.

The current traditional model of public schools is failing our students in many ways. One needs to look no further than their own district's data to see the patterns that the same subgroups are being left behind and this pattern is in essence prohibiting many students from having full access to high levels of academic rigor for which all public schools are responsible for creating.

If one combines looking at academic data with discipline data, it is highly likely to reveal that students of color and special education are suspended disproportionately from their peers. Why do we continue to ignore that public education systems continue to marginalize particular subgroups of our society?

The 2017 Brown Center Report on American Education (Loveless, 2017) and school suspensions informs us, "The U.S. Department of Education's Office for Civil Rights caused a stir in 2014 when it released data showing that black students are suspended and expelled at three times the rate of white students" (p. 23).

Hammond (2015) discusses the *school-to-prison pipeline*:

> Students of color, especially African American and Latino boys, end up spending valuable instructional time in the office rather than the classroom. Consequently, they fall further behind in reading achievement just as reading is becoming the primary tool they will need for taking in new content. Student frustration and shame at being labeled "a slow reader" and having low comprehension lead to more off-task behavior, which the teacher responds to by sending the student out of the classroom. Over time many students of color are pushed out of school because they cannot keep up academically because of poor reading skills and a lack of social-emotional support to deal with their increasing frustration. (p. 13)

The Massachusetts State Equity Plan Update (Massachusetts Department of Elementary & Secondary Education, 2018) further supports how labeling students based on socioeconomic status and race contributes to the societal divide between the haves and the have-nots. This report details how economically disadvantaged, students of color, English learners (ELs), and students with disabilities do not have equal access to highly qualified educators. When students do not have equal access to experienced teachers, their learning experiences suffer, and they perform lower than their white peers on standardized tests.

The Massachusetts State Equity Plan Update (Massachusetts Department of Elementary & Secondary Education, 2018) indicates:

- Economically disadvantaged students, students of color, and ELs are disproportionately assigned to an inexperienced teacher (those with fewer than three years' experience) compared to their peers—9 percent, 43 percent, and 39 percent more often, respectively.
- Hispanic or Latino students are 58 percent more likely than white students to be assigned to an inexperienced teacher.
- African American/black students are 47 percent more likely than white students to be assigned to an inexperienced teacher.
- First-year teachers and principals are more likely to work in lower-performing schools and in schools with large proportions of economically disadvantaged students and students of color.

A Case Study

In one low-performing urban district, the second language learners, high-risk, ELL, and special education students were not reaching *proficiency* levels on statewide assessments and attendance was a significant issue for many teachers and students. Yet more than 95 percent of the teachers in this district received a rating of *proficiency* or *exemplary* on their evaluations from their evaluators. A discrepancy was also seen when comparing report card results to standardized assessment results. They had a very high number of honor roll students, yet the standardized assessments demonstrated more than one-third of each grade level was not reaching *proficiency* on either English, mathematics, or science.

This district, like many districts, was stuck in *status quo* of doing the same things over and over again even when the results indicated something was wrong. When nothing is challenged, districts like this one are inadvertently increasing the divide between the *haves* and the *have-nots*. Social justice and civil rights issues come into play.

Robinson's (2017) summation that public schools are failing and "the waste of talent may not be deliberate, but it's systemic" (p. 5) appears to be true. Educators are not doing their jobs if they are not questioning why public education systems are continually failing certain subgroups of students. Educators need to go beyond asking the questions and take action to change the structures in public education so *all* students have the ability to learn and grow in ways to reach their fullest potential.

Summary

Educators are very familiar with the patterns being discussed in this chapter. Yet for some reason, educators are stuck, so the patterns continue and the trajectory for too many students remains limited. As noted, students who lag behind typically fall into one of the subgroups discussed in this chapter—economically disadvantaged, special education, second language learner, or a minority status.

These students often struggle with basic reading skills, have difficulty keeping up with the learning pace set forth by the classroom teacher, and they fall further and further behind. Many of these students become frustrated and quite often they simply give up. Some students engage in disruptive behaviors that get them sent out of the classroom, while other students learn to become quiet "wall-flowers" and get passed along from grade to grade, even though they are not reaching grade-level mastery.

Hammond (2015) reminds us:

> By third grade, many culturally and linguistically diverse students are one or more years behind in reading, and they will fall further behind in both advanced reading and content knowledge, because of the system's failure to prevent or close small learning gaps in earlier grades. (p. 31)

Hammond (2015) captures the problem with public education with this statement:

> The reality is that they (students) struggle not because of their race, language, or poverty. They struggle because we don't offer them sufficient opportunities in the classroom to develop the cognitive skills and habits of mind that would prepare them to take on more advanced academic tasks. (p. 14)

EDUCATION HAS TO BE TRANSFORMED FROM THE INSIDE OUT

If one were to ask any educator about educational change practices, most educators would say, "We change things all the time in education, and we are doing our very best to meet the needs of *all* learners." While, I agree with this sentiment, I would like to challenge it.

Change

The word *change* is used all too frequently in many schools systems, and as a parent (thirty-three years), educator (twenty years), and a school superintendent (eight years), the challenge is to think about what the word *change* really means for today's educators. In education people often refer to the following kinds of changes:

- grade-level expectations for our students,
- curriculum resources and types of assessments,

- leadership which result in changes in expectations,
- building schedules,
- staffing,
- the demographic makeup of the student population,
- students' academic and social-emotional needs,
- budgets and political climates in our communities, and
- accountability standards at the local, state, and federal levels.

As a verb *change* is defined as *to make different; to make radically different; or to give a different course or direction* (Merriam-Webster, Incorporated, 2018). The word *change* is used incessantly in any given school system, and the true meaning, *to make radically different*, has been watered down to mean something much more surface level by most public educators for a number of reasons. A new superficial definition of the word *change* has emerged in most school organizations for a number of complex internal and external reasons.

Many schools have a culture that is grounded in the tradition of keeping the adult population happy and comfortable. Change practices require the people within the system to have flexible mindsets and the desire to engage in their own productive struggles to learn something new. There are simply not enough people in this category in most schools.

Daily schedules and routines in schools are designed around conformity models where students do what they are told, move from class to class, and respond as critical thinkers or explorers only when they are asked to by their teachers. These limitations hold most school organizations hostage to the *status quo*.

Entitlement

Human beings are creatures of habit. In most public school systems educators, administrators, and teachers alike have been given the *green light* to become very comfortable with the *status quo*, even though many would never admit to this. A colleague once advised to be on the lookout for ROADs, those who are Retired On Active Duty. ROADs are people who are in positions of power simply because of their longevity in a system. They are resistant to do anything outside of their own comfort zone and act as if they are retired but receive a full paycheck.

Unexpectedly a ROAD was detected at a conference in a casual conversation. This teacher was simply asked how he was doing, and he robustly shouted, "I am counting the days!" After hearing this, the group of people around him immediately responded, "We had no idea you were retiring this year." He chuckled loudly and proudly stated, "I'm not retiring this year, but I am retiring next year and just counting my days."

This brief conversation demonstrates how ROADs believe they have earned the right to be blatantly open about their noncommittal stance to invest time, energy, and an authentic passion into educating our students, let alone each individual student. The fact is, in most public school systems once teachers have become tenured, some have been given the green light to become entitled because their job is protected. It is important to stress that tenured teachers are not the problem; the system itself is broken.

Tenured teachers can become less and less concerned with the evaluations from their supervisors, because all they have to do is wait three years and a new principal will appear with a new set of priorities and expectations. This high turnover rate with school leaders adds to the level of resistance from teachers to try new things. After all, how effective is it when schools are constantly shifting priorities and change initiatives with every passing leader that comes and stays for three years? Unfortunately, the *status quo* culture is reinforced every time a new initiative is dismissed and another one is started.

REVOLVING INITIATIVES OR PROFESSIONAL RESPONSIBILITIES?

Ask any educator about the number of new initiatives they are rolling out, and most will breathe a heavy sigh, and then complain about all the extra work they have to do with keeping up with new initiatives. Looking closely at some of the typical *new* initiatives educators are being tasked with, one would discover they fall into the category of normal professional responsibilities:

- updating curriculum resources,
- using data to analyze instructional practices,
- collaborating with teams,
- creating safe and supportive learning environments,
- working on solutions to attendance and behavior issues,
- planning lessons,
- producing updated curriculum maps,
- reviewing student work, and
- participating in student success team meetings.

As previously discussed, the word *change* has been redesigned by many educators to mean something much more surface level than to *make radically different*. Change for most educators is now defined as anything that they are doing that is different than what they *want* to do. The question is: *How can education truly be transformed from the inside, when so many of the people within the system have fixed mindsets believing that change is already happening, when it is not?*

Admittedly, all public school systems have well-intentioned administrators and teachers, but the reality is there are some administrators and teachers who are not serving their schools and students very well, and they should not be working in the field of education. Unlike some of the tenured teachers who are ineffective, administrators can be removed much easier when they are ineffective. Unfortunately, it takes an act of God and thousands of dollars in legal fees to remove any ineffective tenured teacher. Once a teacher is tenured, they have earned a protected status in any public school system, regardless of how well they do their job.

Unfortunately, for our students, there are more and more tenured teachers moving into that comfortable position where they openly choose to do *just enough to get by*. Far too many tenured teachers are openly and actively seeking to earn that ROAD position of power, where they can speak freely about their noncommittal stance toward helping children learn and grow. This pattern feeds a *status quo* culture.

New teachers coming into the teaching profession are watching how some tenured teachers have earned the power to choose how much work they will do in any given day, and they start to emulate this entitlement mindset as well. When you add an ineffective administrator or superintendent into this mix, one can easily see that transformation from inside the system is very difficult to achieve. The prevailing culture in most school organizations protects adults who choose the state of mediocrity and are unwilling to challenge *status quo*.

Ineffective leaders coupled with the entitlement mindset of some tenured teachers are foundational reasons why *status quo* is so difficult to change in today's public schools. The reason success for *all* students is not a true priority in most public schools is directly related to the fixed mindsets of the adults in the system.

Too many adults in any given public school do not want to change their day-to-day routines, schedules, or instructional practices, because they are comfortable, and any change to their routines, schedules, or instructional practices initiate stress. *Status quo* is the result of fixed mindsets and, unfortunately, fixed mindsets are rewarded and protected by tenure in most public school systems.

Although this is the case, the truth is most schools are filled with caring people, who have simply fallen into a trap of doing the same thing as everyone else and that is, *just doing enough to get by*. Transforming public school environments so the majority of administrators, teachers, and students are inspired to think creatively and act differently than most of their peers may sound easy, but it is not.

If public schools are not transformed, masses of students will continue to learn that all they have to do is *just enough to get by*. The cycle of *status quo* teaches our students that mediocrity is rewarded and accepted in our society.

What Can We Do?

The steps to transforming public education begin with closely examining the school culture, spoken and unspoken core values, student achievement data, and discipline data, and working with others to create a clear vision for how *equity for all students* will be protected. This work is hard. It involves building trusting relationships through transparent and ongoing communications with students, families, teachers, staff, administrators, and community members.

While the following steps outline an approach, it is important to note they are not consecutive steps. Rather they are broad concepts that are intertwined and complex. Improving practices involves an ongoing and reflective process where quantifiable data are examined in relationship to any school's climate and culture. People who transform schools:

- listen to various perspectives and solutions while observing day-to-day business practices;
- challenge *status quo* and the fixed mindsets, conscious and unconscious biases that interfere with protecting all students' rights to grow and learn;
- build distributive leadership teams that assist with setting specific goals and measuring the progress of meeting these goals that are aligned to ensuring equitable access for all students;
- model honesty, integrity, and a commitment to empower all stakeholders to use their voices in the ongoing process of change; and
- create and implement action plans that address *status quo*, inequality, discrimination, labeling and tracking students, ineffective instructional programs and practices, outdated curriculum, and ineffective leaders and teachers.

Much like our students, if teachers feel supported and safe, they do take the risks associated with learning something new, and they are more likely to invest authentic energy into implementing change initiatives with fidelity. When leaders set high expectations and model supportive learning environments for teachers, then teachers do the same for their students.

In order to transform schools from the inside out, leaders, teachers, students, families, and community members need to work collaboratively, and, they need to prioritize programs and practices that benefit students. This is truly hard work, and, it only works when we collectively put students' needs before adults' needs. This requires a major mindset shift for many people in school organizations.

Research-Based Instructional Practices

Teachers who consistently use research-based best strategies have the ability to create more flexible learning environments for their students to thrive. In order to radically change the public education system, the real work has to start from inside each and every classroom. An article titled *32 Research-Based Instructional Strategies* (TeachThought Staff, 2017) presents a list of thirty-two concrete actions and strategies. Some of these actions include:

- setting objectives,
- reinforcing effort/providing recognition,
- cooperative learning,
- cues, questions, and advance organizers,
- nonlinguistic representations,
- summarizing and note-taking,
- identifying similarities and differences,
- generating and testing hypotheses,
- rewards based on a specific performance standard,
- direct instruction, and
- scaffolding instruction.

Teachers have the real power to impact radical change. Yet most teachers do not recognize they are in positions to create powerful change. Maybe if teachers were given more time to reflect and learn about the negative system-wide patterns that currently exist in school organizations, they would discover new ways to stop the negative cycle that evolves from labeling students by test scores.

Maybe if leaders and teachers rolled their sleeves up and worked side by side, students' needs and equitable opportunities for all would be prioritized. Maybe if students had a voice in their learning process and were given daily opportunities to engage in untimed productive struggles, where teachers encouraged them to learn from their mistakes, teachers would learn more about their students' learning preferences.

The truth is any radical transformation within public education is not possible without an open examination of both the mindsets of the adults in the system and their day-to-day actions. If the majority of the adults in any school organization are not willing to dig deep to challenge how their own actions and beliefs have contributed to creating a broken system, then real sustainable and radical change is not possible.

As previously noted, teachers have the most power to impact the trajectory of learning for the students they serve. If all teachers were to consistently implement research-based strategies, they would be moving away from the antiquated conformity model that currently exists in most classrooms.

Research-based strategies and practices promote critical thinking, creativity, and put the learner in a position as the explorer. Research-based strategies also provide time for student discourse. When students talk about what they are learning, the information has a better chance of making it into their long-term memory (Sousa, 2016).

Leaders

Research-based strategies are not reserved for teachers alone. Leaders also need to consider the best practices they need to implement on a daily basis to eradicate *status quo* and mediocracy. Leaders also need to have flexible mindsets, and high levels of engagement, to see change initiatives grow into sustainable routines. Leaders need to align budgets to support the ongoing use of research-based materials in classrooms. Leaders need to promote an inquiry-based culture for the adults. Leaders need to model that change efforts focused on ensuring all students have equitable access to discover their individual talents are worth the work.

Education needs more leaders across the board—not just superintendents or principals. Schools need teacher leaders. Schools need student leaders. Schools need parent leaders. And, schools need community leaders. All these leaders need to collaborate to eliminate the mediocracy that exists in public education today.

To accomplish these goals, here is a list of best practices for any leader who has the courage to act as change-agent on behalf of the students we serve:

1. Be transparent about *why* there is a need for change and transformation.
2. Pay particular attention to *equity*, when analyzing any situation, building schedules, student achievement data, student programming, evaluations, curriculum resources, and the unspoken core values of the school community.
3. Pay particular attention to mindsets of the people within the organization, including your own mindset.
4. Model collaboration, creative thinking, and taking an action-based approach.
5. Provide supports and guidelines for change initiatives and be willing to be flexible with how things evolve.
6. Establish multiple ways for two-way communications and be open to ongoing feedback.

7. Build trust through meaningful relationships and common goals.
8. Build a climate of inquiry.
9. Be clear that *status quo* will be confronted.

Superintendent's Level of Engagement

The Gallup 2017 Superintendent Survey of K-12 School District Superintendents, titled *Leadership Perspectives on Public Education* (Gallup, Inc., 2017), provides some interesting statistics regarding a superintendent's level of engagement in their districts. This study defined engagement as "a measure of the extent to which workers are psychologically committed and emotionally connected to their role as a result of having their performance-related needs met" (Gallup, Inc., 2017, p. 4). As Sousa (2016) points out, emotions are connected to learning, and interestingly, superintendents, like students and teachers, are most engaged when they are emotionally connected.

This Gallup 2017 Superintendent Survey (Gallup, Inc.) involved 12,432 K-12 school superintendents and focused on how they perceived how their roles impacted their own level of engagement, and how their levels of engagement then impacted the expectations they set forth for the people working in their districts. The results indicated only "42% of public K–12 superintendents are engaged at work, while 52% are not engaged and 6% are actively disengaged" (p. 4).

With only 42% of our superintendents engaged in their work, we need to ask: *How does a superintendent's engagement level impact the development and sustainability of transformational change?* If a superintendent is engaged, do change initiatives have a higher chance of succeeding? If a superintendent is not engaged, how likely is it that *status quo* will continue to thrive across a district?

CONCLUSIONS

Public education can only be transformed from the inside when teachers and leaders are working in unison to challenge how their own attitudes and beliefs contribute to *status quo* and mediocrity. Once there is a level of synergy between teachers and leaders, they can make a conscious decision as a team to unleash their creativity with the sole purpose of creating new structures and new systems of support for *all* students.

Equity for all students needs to be the driving force for transformational change. Building consensus for change takes time, trust, and honesty. Communication is the key, and all parties need to practice reflection and *productive struggles* when trying to come up with new innovative ideas. From one superintendent's perspective, change requires people to have flexible mindsets and high levels of emotional intelligence, so they can help create safe environments to afford *everyone* the ability to use their voices.

Transformational change can take place gradually, in one classroom at a time, with one teacher at a time, and with one leader at a time. The important piece to consider is whether or not the change is really transformational or simply another version of what is already being done. Transformational change involves reflection, data analysis, and critical feedback.

As previously discussed, challenging *status quo* requires people to have difficult conversations about how they define success; how they will ensure all students have opportunities to thrive and flourish as independent thinkers; and how they will change their own day-to-day actions and beliefs. The discussions on *how* structures and procedures need to change must be clear to everyone. The action plans of *what* people will do differently to ensure *equity* for all students need to be measurable. And, finally a *cycle* of following up on how the plan is going is an essential part of making ongoing improvements that lead to transformations in school organizations.

It takes courage and a lot of energy to fight *status quo* culture that exists in too many public school systems. There are leaders, teachers, and schools where changing *status quo* from the inside out is occurring. Thus, changing *status quo* is doable, yet very difficult to sustain. To transform public education from the inside out, the adults within public education systems need to start by looking in the mirror. *we* need to demonstrate through our words, beliefs, and day-to-day actions that *we* truly enjoy the hard work of holding each other accountable to become the *best* advocates possible for *all* the students *we* serve.

Change Is Possible

In one urban district serving more than 50 percent economically disadvantaged students, transformational change from the inside out is occurring. In the high school, the mathematics teachers are actively working on changing their own mindsets and teaching styles as they implement a new program, the College Preparatory Mathematics (CPM) program. These teachers are incorporating new strategies in their classrooms that are much more activity-based and student-focused. Students are able to work in groups and on project-based assignments.

The hands-on activities have assisted with ensuring all students are engaged in ways that push them to deeply understand the mathematical concepts they are learning. The shift in how the teachers were teaching mathematics has been so dramatic that students rebelled against it. The students wanted things to go back to "normal" where the teachers simply gave them the answer and showed them the formula to memorize.

The shifts in these teachers' mindsets have resulted in them placing higher expectations on their students. These higher expectations have transformed the mathematics classroom environments at this school. These mathematics teachers are modeling ongoing reflection and their own *productive struggles* with learning something new. Instead of assisting students by simply telling them the right answer, now students work independently or in groups to discover the answers.

A major paradigm shift has occurred. Classrooms that used to have rows of desks now have group tables for collaborative work. Students who were expected to conform and sit in rows are now moving around the classroom freely talking about mathematics. Teachers, who stood in front of the class doing all the talking, are now rotating from table to table to observe how their students are figuring out what they are learning.

Change is possible, and it has to start somewhere. The adults in public schools need to be reflective practitioners and take ownership for how their day-to-day actions have contributed to the negative results we see in too many public schools. After taking ownership, we need to take action and follow up on our actions to ensure we are really making changes to tackle *status quo*.

Together, educators in public schools have the talents, intelligence, knowledge, and skills to transform their schools from the inside out. We just need the courage to begin, and the desire to do the hard work, to change ourselves on behalf of the students we serve. If *status quo* continues, today's educators will be to blame for the broader gaps in our society between the *haves* and the *have-nots*.

In an ideal world, all educators want the best for their students. Here is the challenge for all educators:

> As a professional educator you are charged and empowered to educate and inspire *all* students. The future of our democratic society and the future path of the students you serve is dependent upon how you relate to, support, and inspire each and every one of your students. Your unconscious biases are speaking loudly and clearly to you, every time you or your school labels a student as "difficult," "low performer," or "unreachable." Remember, your day-to-day reactions to your students can either inspire or crush them. Be kind with your words and actions. Be an advocate for *all* students regardless of their needs. Be persistent and focused on figuring out what strategies work best for each and every one of your students. Change is possible in public education, and it starts when you have the courage to challenge and reflect upon how your own beliefs, attitudes, and day-to-day actions impact your students. You can create change because you are a professional educator. Go for it and challenge the systems that are outdated and broken!

Chapter 6

What Next: Boom or Bust

Carlton J. Fitzgerald and Simona Laurian-Fitzgerald

The authors of this book began the process of discussing the assumptions for this work, knowing how important assumptions are to how people see the world. In this case the world is that of education. After more than twenty-five years of frustration with the lack of effective reform in education, in spite of many valiant efforts, the authors decided to try to do something to help beyond our individual efforts in our schools and districts. The purpose of this book is to help other educators, like us, who have been struggling to help our students make the world a better place.

Like many educators, the group came to the conclusion that educational reform has been ineffective, not because of a lack of effort but rather a lack of the right assumptions upon which to build reform. Those discussions led to the following four assumptions for this book:

1. Our educational systems must be transformed.
2. That transformation should be led by educators.
3. Each student must be valued in every school and in every classroom.
4. Success looks different for each student.

First, each individual author had to admit that education has been built upon the assumptions of the Industrial Revolution, instead of the assumptions of the social, technological, and information realities of an ever-changing world. The world is going to continue to depend more and more on technology for learning, work, leisure, and innovations. Artificial intelligence is going to grow and impact the world in many different ways (Lee, 2019). Global and local social and economic changes will continue to challenge society (Robinson, 2017). Students are either going to be prepared for the new world of work, leisure, global politics, and international business, or they will be left behind.

Second, if we look at the most successful schools and nations, educators and students play critical roles in developing the teaching and learning process (Laurian-Fitzgerald, Popa, Fitzgerald, 2015; Robinson, 2017). Recruiting the best and the brightest students to become teachers is critical to the process. Future educators must be trained extensively and supported as they enter the field of education. Those dedicated educators who already work diligently for their students should be the leaders of the educational transformation movement. Politicians, the community, and state boards should assist and encourage teacher and student leaders in their efforts, not stand in their way.

Third, every student needs to be valued as an important human being who deserves to have a voice in their education, and every student should have adult mentors to help guide their development. The world can no longer afford to have schools generate groups of haves and have-nots. That is just too dangerous a proposition that is already causing havoc all around the world. There are too many stressed or angry or discouraged young people in our nation and the world, and schools have the potential to help change that situation. Schools can and should create environments that are safe and caring and in which students are encouraged to find their voices, interests, and passions.

Fourth, every student does develop and learn differently. Making every student and teacher work in a one-style-fits-all environment makes no sense. Teachers must learn, develop, and implement techniques centered on students and their needs. In order to accomplish that, educators must develop pedagogical and andragogical skills to help move students from receivers of education to developers of learning, from passive observers to active participants, and from dependent learners to independent learners, critical thinkers, and problem solvers. Instead of holding people accountable, education should inspire teachers and students to be joyous, caring, and courageous learners.

These assumptions are not pipe dreams, they are relevant and real assumptions that, if brought to life, will encourage educators to help all students reach their potentials. It is time for educators and students to take back education. There are many excuses as to why this might be too difficult, but the time for excuses has come and gone. Thousands of teachers have already begun this process; the time is ripe, but if we do not take advantage of the present opportunities to transform education, the opportunities will be lost. Educators have a choice to make: allow non-educators to continue to mandate what schools do or take back education and do what is right for our students.

The authors of this book have described the following ways in which they have begun to attempt to make teaching and learning more student-focused:

- do away with exams,
- have students and teachers codevelop classes,
- partner with the community,
- empower teachers and students,
- purposefully work to put students first,
- help students explore their interests, and
- change our roles from disseminators to advisors.

It will be messy, and teachers will make mistakes, but it will also be extremely energizing and fun.

This chapter discusses ten ideas intended to help teachers think about student-centered teaching and learning:

1. meet student needs;
2. critical thinking;
3. meaningful assessments;
4. universally designed teaching;
5. trauma-sensitive teaching;
6. culturally-response teaching;
7. experiences in complex projects;
8. teach positive social skills to make students good teammates;
9. help students find their interests, talents, and passions; and
10. personalize education.

These ideas are not exhaustive, they are just some ways for people to approach putting students at the center of the learning process. There are many other ideas in the field for becoming more student-centered. The goal in this chapter is to help people who are looking for ways to be more student-centered to find techniques that fit with their philosophy of teaching.

The chapter will end with a discussion of how superintendents and/or principals might develop ideas to supervise teachers in teacher-centered ways. The process works better if principals treat teachers with the same care and respect for their talents and passions they want teachers to employ with their students. Teachers need encouragement and support to take risks as they learn new ways to encourage and support their students. As the why, what, and how of teaching changes, the why, what, and how of supervision of teachers also must change.

Need-Fulfilling Environments

In a student-centered classroom, teachers purposefully and strategically attempt to help students meet as many needs as possible: emotional, psychological, social, intellectual, and physical. How teachers define the needs is not as important as the fact that they have a set of needs in mind as they create the classroom environment, how they treat students, how they teach students to treat each other, and how they help students become competent and passionate people.

There are at least the following six basic needs teachers can help students meet:

1. emotional and physical survival and safety;
2. love and belonging;
3. power, significance, and competence;
4. freedom to make decisions;
5. fun and joyfulness; and
6. meaningfulness (Fitzgerald, 2003; Fitzgerald & Laurian, 2013; Glasser, 1998, 2006; Maslow, 1970, 1971).

Helping students meet their needs allows educators to work with students in powerful ways that go far beyond what we do when we make students comply in schools.

When students feel safe and secure, when they feel loved and cared for, when they have a voice, when they feel important and competent, when they make important decisions about their learning, when they feel joy, and when they are sharing important and meaningful experiences, they do not comply with the school rules; they embody the rules of decency, love, and caring; and learning becomes a personal and important journey for them. They are becoming the people they are meant to be and that motivates them to search for and develop their talents, creativity, and curious nature. They are not mandated to learn, they are inspired to learn.

This process can begin with teaching students how to treat each other in a safe and caring environment. Teachers ensure their space is safe physically and emotionally. For example, teachers ensure their rooms and other places they supervise are bully-free zones. This includes the ways teachers discipline their students. Discipline, in this philosophy, is taught, not dispensed. Children learn to bully, and they can learn better ways to get their needs met. Teachers take their role of supervisor seriously, and intentionally are visible and alert to how students are treating each other. In class, these teachers teach prosocial skills to all students.

When incidents occur, teachers deal with them in firm, fair, and consistently peaceful ways that keep all students safe, while teaching students to improve their social skills. The attitude behind the interactions among everyone in class is to be supportive and caring. Teachers help students learn how to be caring, supportive, encouraging, trustworthy, good listeners, negotiators, and positive people who contribute to their class and classmates. Teachers at every level can develop a specific set of social skills they want for their students (e.g., saying please and thank you, encouraging their peers, being active listeners, negotiating differences).

Students in these student-centered classes work with their peers on a regular basis, so they can practice their prosocial skills, and their teachers give feedback and assistance when needed. Teachers and students might create sayings for their class, like: *In our classroom, we care for and about each other all of the time.* Like any other skills, good citizenship takes practice, feedback, new learning, and more practice and feedback. Physically and emotionally safe classrooms do not happen by accident; teachers set the positive tone and help their students to become competent in creating a safe environment with and for each other.

Creating a safe environment is made stronger by helping students understand that people in school care about them, and they are allowed to care about each other. One way that teachers can facilitate the need for love and belonging is through the use of base groups (Johnson & Johnson, 2009). Teachers form base groups so that students can encourage each other academically and personally. The base group is a long-lasting group (e.g., for a year or more) in which the teacher develops opportunities for the students to get to know each other and to help each other.

It is very important that every student feels like they belong in the classroom and school. By celebrating (e.g., birthdays, end of the term) together and doing projects together (e.g., community service, service learning), students develop connections to each other and with their teacher. When students help each other (e.g., prepare for exams, complete a writing project), they build positive relationships in school. The goal is to make sure every student feels accepted in school.

One way for teachers to help students feel accepted is to give students opportunities to create their voices. The need for power (or the feeling that what one thinks matters) is a vital need in all human beings, and when teachers help students develop their own voices, it is a very powerful message to students: *What you think matters, you matter.* When teachers can add techniques to help students be successful (e.g., scaffolding, universally designed experiences, using students' strengths to learn), then students can be motivated to tackle new and challenging material, because they know their teachers and peers will help them succeed.

When teachers purposefully help students have fun in school, while engaging in meaningful work, teaching and learning become acts of pride and joy. That does not mean people do not work hard; when people are having fun and doing things that matter to them, they almost always work harder. Why do students work so hard, and why are they so dedicated to their cocurricular activities? They choose their activities, often out of one of their passions; they are expected to do their best; they are given positive and helpful feedback; they are given regular opportunities for practice and/or rehearsal; and they are part of something that is extremely important to them. They are getting their needs met in positive ways.

If teachers and students can meet their basic needs in school in positive ways, they will much more likely want to be in school, work hard, be engaged and enthusiastic, and motivated to teach and learn. When incidences arise, people will work through the issues in much more cooperative and positive ways. The culture of the school will be transformed because students and staff will feel supported, cared about, competent, important, and joyful because they will understand that each person matters. They will also know that the work they are being asked to do is important work that will help them in the real world.

Critical Thinking

Another approach to student-centered teaching and helping students to prepare themselves for life after graduation is through critical thinking. One of the goals of student-centered teaching and learning is to help students move from being dependent learners to become independent learners. In order to become independent learners, students must be able to think critically. Students will only become critical thinkers if they are given regular opportunities to develop critical-thinking skills. When teachers control the teaching and learning process, then teachers are doing all or most of the critical thinking. The control must be shifted more and more to students.

There are some different approaches teachers can use with and for students. A common approach is to develop assignments for students using a critical-thinking model like Bloom's *Taxonomy* (Bloom, 1956; Sousa, 2017). This process deals with learning on two domains: the cognitive and the knowledge. In other words, all learning requires that students use different levels of thinking and different levels of knowledge. The cognitive process dimension has students think at six different levels (see table 6.1).

In this process, students also have to gain knowledge, and they have to learn something. In the knowledge dimension of learning there are at least four elements to knowledge that also move from more concrete to more abstract (see table 6.2): (1) factual, (2) conceptual, (3) procedural, and (4) metacognitive.

Table 6.1 Cognitive Processes

Cognitive Process	Kinds/Levels of Thinking
Remember	Identify, recognize, recall: define, list, name, label
Understand	Explain, interpret, classify, summarize: explain, describe, illustrate
Apply	Implement, carry out: complete, solve, use, demonstrate
Analyze	Distinguish, differentiate, integrate, structure: compare and contrast, break down, integrate
Evaluate	Judge, test, assess, monitor, critique: justify, recommend, relate
Create	Make, develop, hypothesize, construct: design, establish, invent

Sources: Bloom (1956) and Sousa (2017).

Table 6.2 Knowledge Dimension of Learning

Knowledge Dimension	Elements of Each Dimension
Factual	Vocabulary, details, components/elements
Procedural	Subject-specific: Skills, techniques, methods, algorithms; knowing when to use each
Conceptual	Categories, classifications, principles, theories, models
Metacognitive	Self-knowledge: How one thinks; how one learns

It makes sense to attempt to have all students think and learn at every level. Students should experience work at each level of thinking and learning, and they should be assessed at the different cognitive and learning levels. In other words, students should experience the curriculum and be assessed (formatively and summatively) on at least three levels of thinking and understanding. Cognitively students can be assessed at their levels of processing: (1) remember and understand, (2) apply and analyze, and (3) evaluate and create. At the knowledge domain, students can be assessed at the following levels: (1) factual, (2) procedural and conceptual, and (3) metacognitive.

These levels give teachers a much more accurate way to assess students than is accomplished with a single-element assessment. It is not as important what specific critical-thinking model a teacher uses, as it is to use a model. There are alternative models available (e.g., "Depth of knowledge," in Webb, 2002; "Six facets," in Wiggins & McTighe, 2005).

Richard Andrusiak (chapter 3) writes about the importance of habits of mind in learning. The point is to have students use critical-thinking habits of mind on a regular basis. Carlton Fitzgerald and Simona Laurian-Fitzgerald (chapter 1) discuss aspects of critical thinking. Table 6.3 is the authors' version for a model of critical thinking that with practice and rehearsal can become habits for students (and teachers). In order to develop the acquisition of habits of mind, students have to be given ongoing opportunities and positive feedback on a regular basis. Students must be challenged by their

Table 6.3 Critical-Thinking Habits

Thinking Skills/Habits	Actions of Critical Thinkers
Independent	Listen to others, gather information, make up one's own mind
Ego-centered; group-centered	Understand the difference between not listening to anyone else and/or always believing what the group says
Open-minded	Try to understand other perspectives; assess other perspectives based on the merit of their logic and facts
Metacognitive	Learn about oneself; expose one's own assumptions; assess why one feels as they do; assess how feelings effect one's thinking
Humble	Learn that other ideas are worthy of study. Add to one's knowledge when new ideas make sense
Courageous	Remember there are times when people fear hearing new and different ideas. Be ready to positively challenge the *status quo*
Honorable	Try to do the right things for the right reasons. Believe other people are trying to do the same
Determined	Finding the best resolutions to issues often require persistence, time, and great effort
Confident	When one develops ideas using these and other habits of mind, maintain confidence in one's work

teachers and peers on a regular basis to demonstrate and defend their observations and opinions.

Students must work on real-world (or simulated real-world) issues and problems regularly, if they are going to develop these attitudes and skills. Real-world problems are often too complicated and too important to allow an individual to work alone. That is why most nations, companies, and institutions put people on teams to solve complex and important issues. In classes, students should develop the prosocial skills to work as teammates and the critical-thinking attitudes and skills to become effective problem solvers.

Caine (2018) explains that teachers and students should develop "complex immersion" experiences in which students have to be persistent, creative, and skillful as they struggle to find resolutions to meaningful and complex issues. Richard Andrusiak (chapter 3) describes how he employs "open projects" with his students to integrate teaching of mathematics with students' majors or interests.

Whatever critical habits or skills one believes in, the teacher should strategically help students acquire the critical-thinking knowledge and skills, and then help students turn the knowledge and skills into habits through rehearsal and practice (Sousa, 2017). Any skill develops over time going through the skill acquisition processes: (1) awareness, (2) initial skill-building, (3) guided skill-building, (4) independent practice, and (5) independent competence. If every teacher in every grade level chose a few skills to work on each year, students would be proficient critical thinkers by graduation.

Meaningful Assessments

All of the authors in this book, in one way or another, have discussed meaningfulness as an important element of student-centered teaching and learning. In chapter 2, Christopher Geraghty discusses how students and teachers are begging for more meaningful work in schools. Richard Andrusiak (chapter 3) is advocating for eliminating exams for gateway classes, and he is looking for ways to do the same for most classes.

Amana Bastoni (chapter 4) is working hard to make more meaningful connections between academic classes and technical classes. How, she asks, can students truly be career ready when classroom work is so disconnected in so many schools? Ruthann Petruno-Goguen (chapter 5) describes how she has witnessed too many students being left behind because the work they are asked to accomplish makes little sense to so many students.

An important aspect of meaningful work is assessment. If the goals of education include creating positive and educated citizens and workers who want to make the world a better place, then our assessment practices should mirror those goals. Assessments must do more than give students grades or competency level scores. The authors of this book have advocated for assessing students in at least three levels of knowledge and thinking. Schools should know what their students know (knowledge), how well they can critically think (cognition), and what they can do (performance). Assessments that narrow those important elements of learning shortchange our teachers and students.

Thus, assessment plans should evaluate students at different levels and for each of the three elements of learning. Some basic questions for an assessment plan might include:

1. What do our students know and understand?
2. How effectively can students apply what they know and understand?
3. How effectively can students use the knowledge and skills they have acquired to solve new problems, questions, situations, and/or initiatives?

These three questions could be asked for each of the three elements of learning (i.e., knowledge, cognition, and performance). School assessments should be able to allow teachers to assess curriculum competencies, college competencies, career competencies, and critical-thinking competencies from both an academic perspective and a real-world perspective.

Most importantly, teachers and students will feel that their work is worthwhile, because assessments will be real and meaningful for everyone.

Naturally, the more assessments can be personalized and/or designed with individual students, the more meaningful assessments will be for students. If teachers assess students and students self-assess in multiple ways and at multiple levels, they will be able to gather a more complete and accurate picture of learning.

According to Sousa (2017), it is important to personalize assessments for students. Students should be able to demonstrate what they have learned and can do in ways that make the most sense to the students. For example, an artistic student may do much better using art media to demonstrate their knowledge and skills. Richard Andrusiak (chapter 3) discusses open projects, in which the professor/teacher and the student work together to integrate disciplines into projects designed collaboratively between the student and the professor/teacher. The products and process are codeveloped so that students are using their strengths and passions to develop their work and assessments.

According to constructionism theory, an important part of this process is student public presentation of their work. Students work on real issues or complex questions, and they are required to present their final products, findings, and/or recommendations in public forums, hopefully to a real audience. Papert and Harel (1991) define constructionism:

> Constructionism—the N (noun) word as opposed to the V (verb) word—shares constructivism's connotation of learning as "building knowledge structures" irrespective of the circumstances of the learning. It then adds the idea that this happens especially felicitously in a context where the learner is consciously engaged in constructing a public entity, whether it's a sand castle on the beach or a theory of the universe. (p. 1)

According to Quaglia (2014) student choice and voice are integral to the learning process. This includes the creation of meaningful self-assessment practices throughout the learning process. Student-centered assessments are at the core of meaningful and thorough assessments. The goal should be, according to Quaglia (2014), Caine (2018), and Sousa (2017), to give students as much authority as possible in this process. The teacher role changes to that of mentor, guide, and/or facilitator. The teacher is the master educator helping all students move from novice learners to master learners.

Another advantage of using a student-centered process like project-based learning is that it becomes easier and more natural to integrate learning. Richard Andrusiak (chapter 3) and Christopher Geraghty (chapter 2) both discuss the importance of integration in their chapters. Their ideas make a great deal of sense because, if we are serious about helping students own their learning, educators must strategically give voice, authority, and responsibility to the students.

The process is similar no matter the circumstances (e.g., master electrician to novice electrician, master doctor to intern, advisor to advisee, master to apprentice). The goal is for the master mentor to guide the novitiate from beginner to expert, from novice to master, from intern to doctor, from dependent learner to independent learner. If the learning process is a combination of learning, assessment, and feedback, more learning, more assessment, and more feedback, until mastery, then how students are assessed must change. It must change from an accountability process to a learning process, centered on the student.

Universally Designed Learning Activities

The philosophy behind student-centered learning believes that every student is capable and should be assisted to become a successful learner. It is common knowledge that people process information and learn skills differently. Most teachers are familiar with the theory of Multiple Intelligences (Gardner, 2011) that proposes people have at least nine intelligences that they use in the real world. People see the world differently based on their life experiences and how they process information. Yet in many places all students are expected to learn the same things in the same ways and be assessed using a one-size-fits-all assessment.

In a student-centered process, teachers use their understandings about physical, emotional, and social development, cognitive processing, emotional states, physical differences, and personal backgrounds and worldviews to develop learning experiences that directly connect with all students. At the least, this means that teachers must develop multiple ways for students to process knowledge, interact with curriculum, and demonstrate what they have learned.

A universal design philosophy believes that each student should be taught, interact with the material being learned, and produce proof of learning in ways that work for the student. Novak (2016) defines universal design for teaching and learning as "thoroughly knowing the concept you're going to teach and presenting that concept in different ways while engaging the students and encouraging them to express their knowledge in different ways" (p. 13). The point of universal design is to proactively and strategically eliminate barriers to learning so all students can successfully access the curriculum.

For student-centered teachers, this is an issue of equity. Raising the standards in this philosophy means creating and implementing learning experiences in which all people learn important curriculum and skills. Remember, one of the assumptions for this book is all students are important. This means teachers have to adapt what they do with and for students. For far too long, the only people adapting in education have been the students. It is the teacher, the expert, the master, the professional educator, who needs to ensure that all students can and do access the learning.

From a deficit model or mindset for teaching, teachers believe that some students simply do not have what it takes to be successful, and they believe teaching cannot change that. So, these teachers lower their expectations for themselves and their students. If teachers remove barriers to learning, many of the excuses for failure disappear, and teachers can challenge all of their students to achieve.

Universal design is based on three teaching guidelines (CAST, 2018). They include providing multiple means for (1) engagement, (2) representation, and (3) action and expression. The idea is to engage students, present curriculum, have students work with the curriculum, and display learning in a variety of ways, so all students can access the curriculum and learn successfully. Table 6.4 displays some ideas connected to the guidelines created by CAST.

A major concept in the universal design process is student choice. As students learn about themselves as learners, they will be able to choose the best alternatives for their learning. Students will need time to try out different ways to process information, work with the curriculum, and communicate their learning to teachers. Along the way, teachers should help students

Table 6.4 Ways to Develop Equity in Teaching and Learning

	Universal Design Ideas	
Engagement	Representation	Action and Expression
Recruit interest, hook students in, engage students in meaningful work	Consider how different students perceive and process information; use a variety of ways for students to perceive curriculum	Set up experiences with multiple physical actions; employ all of the senses
Sustain effort and persistence, teach to student strengths, scaffold learning, encourage making errors	Make language and symbols accessible (e.g., preteach, review, practice, and rehearse); ensure required prerequisite knowledge and skills exist	Promote multiple ways for students to express their ideas and learning; encourage cooperative learning so students communicate their learning; develop student voice
Provide options for self-regulation and student choice; help students find their voice	Comprehension—match presentation styles with learning abilities, readiness, interests, etc.; give accurate and helpful feedback; chunk learning	Enhance student executive function; engage students in teams and in complex projects; teach and model problem-solving and critical thinking

Sources: CAST (2018); Johnson and Johnson (2009); Novak (2016); Quaglia (2014); and Sousa (2017).

reflect on what is working and what is not working for them. It is important for teachers to believe that, if they provide good options and scaffold the work, students will succeed.

Scaffolding is the process where teachers give students the help they need to be successful, and, as the students become more competent, gradually releasing the support until the students can work independently. The idea behind scaffolding is to give students only the help they need and to remove the assistance when students are ready to work on their own.

According to Puntambekar and Hübscher (2005), scaffolding is an interactive process between the teacher and the student, so that they work together to determine progress and needs. The authors describe four important ingredients of scaffolding:

1. intersubjectivity: a shared understanding of the task that has been co-redefined by the teacher and the student;
2. teacher-created appropriate help based on ongoing diagnosis of student understanding, allowing the teacher to offer different types of graduated assistance;
3. active engagement between the teacher and the student; and
4. fading support and transfer of control from teacher control, to co-control, to student control.

From a universal design perspective, teachers attempt to proactively build in scaffolding into the normal process of teaching and learning. As teachers learn from their students what kinds of assistance different students need, they will be more prepared to build those typical forms of scaffolding into their regular systems of teaching. Teachers are finding that, as they build in variety as recommended in the three principles of universal design ([1] engagement, [2] representation, and [3] action and expression), most students take advantage of the options, not just students with identified needs. In other words, universal design is helpful—universally.

Trauma-Sensitive Teaching

According to Jennings (2019) students with trauma are becoming more evident in our schools. Bullying is once again on the rise in our nation, the opioid epidemic in our nation is causing many families to experience trauma, poverty negatively effects millions of students, racism and other forms of prejudice are causing many to deal with trauma, and there is a rise in post-traumatic stress syndrome for soldiers and their families from the effects of wars in the Middle East. Schools are also experiencing an influx of immigrant students, many of whom have experienced trauma in their lives. Jennings explains that trauma causes many students to have difficulties in school academically, socially, and emotionally. Often the typical policies in schools treat students of trauma in the opposite fashion with which they should be treated. Instead of being punished, students of trauma need assistance to deal with their complex issues.

Trauma results from:

> an event, series of events, or set of circumstances that is experienced by an individual as physically or emotionally harmful or life threatening and that has lasting adverse effects on the individual's functioning and mental, physical, social, emotional, or spiritual well-being. (SAMSHA as cited in Jennings, 2019, p. 9)

Part of the issue with students is that most are too young and/or inexperienced to understand how to deal with their issues. Many adults have difficulties in dealing with their trauma, and young people have fewer experiences and understandings to try to deal with trauma.

It is important for a teacher to be aware that a student might be affected by trauma. One problem is that many of the signs of trauma look like other issues: inability to focus, uncooperative in their work groups, inattentive in class, argumentative or defiant, jumpy or nervous, has a self-protective attitude, tired most of the time, dramatic, or disheveled or dirty. These signs could be connected to different issues, and when a teacher observes them on a regular basis, it is a sign that something is going on that is not good. It is important for the teacher to do some research (e.g., read records, talk with previous teachers, talk with a school counselor).

A teacher does not necessarily need to know the specifics, but it is important to realize that something is amiss for the student. No matter the issues, students need assistance in school to be successful. In order to help students be more successful in school, teachers can think about what Jennings (2019) calls the keys to compassionate teaching:

1. helping students build supportive relationships with teachers and peers,
2. creating a safe and caring learning environment with consistent routines and procedures that move past historical stereotypes and biases and support student empowerment, voice, and choice, and
3. building upon strengths by supporting the development of self-regulation. (p. 47)

One step is to help students create and sustain positive relationships in school. Students of trauma often need to see how people function in positive relationships. It is important for teachers to build a positive relationship with a student of trauma, and it is important for the teacher to help students maintain positive relationships in class. Teaching students prosocial skills is important; teaching students how to resolve conflicts in positive ways is important; and making sure students understand they are worthwhile and that the teacher will not give up on them is important.

A second step is to create a class climate in which all people feel safe physically and emotionally. Students of trauma often feel like they are outsiders—they are different from everyone else. It is important to develop classrooms in which everyone is accepted for who they are. Students need to know in this class everyone is important and cared for by the teacher and the students. In a trauma-sensitive classroom, people leave their biases behind when they enter the classroom. As part of the process, the teacher helps each student discover their voice. Students are given authority to make important choices in their class work.

Students who have trauma in their lives often have underdeveloped executive functions. They need help to further develop their abilities to make important decisions and to problem-solve effectively. Stress inhibits a student's ability to make rational decisions (Sousa, 2017), so in the classroom, students should be engaged in negotiating, problem-solving, and critical-thinking experiences in a safe and caring environment. Students should be taught how to self-assess and set goals for themselves. They should be encouraged to learn about themselves as learners.

Above all, teachers should be compassionate with students who struggle in general, but maybe especially with students who have to deal with trauma in their lives. These students have already faced some of the harsh realities of life, what they need now is some compassion to help them know they are valued, normal human beings who deserve a good life. Finally, teachers should not be afraid to ask for help. They should reach out to the principal, school counselor, school psychologist, social worker, and the like. Teachers should help to create a team to help all students who deal with trauma.

Culturally Responsive Teaching

Another important approach for student-centered teaching is culturally responsive teaching. In schools that are becoming more culturally diverse, it is critical to ensure that all students feel welcomed in their classes and schools, and it is important to ensure that all students learn successfully. So, the first thing teachers can do to help their students is to become more aware of the cultural differences in their classes. Once aware, the job for teachers is to develop a culturally diverse curriculum. As in many things teachers do in their classes, when they develop more diverse curricula, it is good for all students.

This is another version of equity in education. If all students are going to be able to connect to their education experiences, then, of course, they need to see themselves in the curriculum. Hammond (2015) writes, "For culturally and linguistically diverse students, their opportunities to develop habits of mind and cognitive capacities are limited or non-existent because of educational inequity" (p. 13). Teachers must be aware of these discrepancies, and they must take positive action to help move all students from being dependent to independent students.

By now, in this book, this should sound familiar. One of the most important goals of any school is to help all students become independent learners. Some themes keep reappearing:

1. create safe and caring environments;
2. scaffold for all students who need assistance;
3. maintain high standards for all students;
4. universally design the curriculum for all students;
5. create positive relationships between the teacher and students and between and among all students;
6. meet the emotional, intellectual, physical, and social needs of all students;
7. ensure every student has a voice;
8. create equity for all students;
9. celebrate diversity; and
10. give progressively more authority and responsibility for learning to the students.

These are the cornerstones of success for all students in school. For each different group of students there are issues to consider, and in this case the differences are cultural.

First, teachers must get to know their students. For culturally diverse students, this means understanding students' cultures. It is not enough to just be a nice person to students, as teachers must help students move from dependence to independence. Every student deserves a rich curriculum, and part of that process is a curriculum that includes all students. Every student should learn about different cultures. When students share their ideas in class or in their writings, they should share their cultural diversity. For example, it is important for teachers to understand that in some cultures their oral traditions are critical to learning.

Storytelling is vital in so many different cultures. Stories bring out the values of the culture; they keep alive important traditions; and they bring people together as a community. As teachers help students develop their voices, storytelling is an important element of that process. Everyone has stories from their cultural backgrounds, and those stories should be fostered in school, not ignored. Sharing each other's stories helps students to feel accepted, and it also helps students hear other perspectives in positive ways. When students listen to each other's stories, they get to know each other better, and they are building appreciation for diversity.

Equity does not mean that the majority accepts the minority. Instead, equity builds up the appreciation and respect for diverse thinking, ways to live, and ways to view the world. This goes beyond accepting, because mere accepting implies there is a more important group and a less important group. Equity means that all people are important, and all people have important things to share about life. The difference between a teacher who has a day for diversity in their class is so different from a teacher who helps students enrich their lives with diverse cultures and perspectives on a regular basis. One accepts diversity, the other embraces diversity.

Second, once teachers know their students, it is important to help the students get to know each other. Sharing their stories is one way to get at that. Creating experiences in which students share their ideas from their perspectives adds to the learning of all students. For example, when reading a poem, putting students into small groups where they have to synthesize their responses by actively listening to each other is an important element of embracing diversity. Integrating diversity into the everyday fabric of learning is important.

Third, teachers have to reflect on themselves and commit to being more diverse in thinking and work. Hammond (2015) states:

> The true power of culturally responsive teaching comes from being comfortable in your own skin because you are not a neutral party in the process. You can never take yourself out of the equation. Instead, you must commit to the journey. This means we each must do the "inside-out" work required: developing the right mindset, engaging in self-reflection, checking our implicit biases, practicing social-emotional awareness, and holding an inquiry stance regarding the impact of our interactions on students. (p. 53)

In order to help students become more open and embracing, teachers have to do the hard work of understanding our own biases and restrictive attitudes. Teachers' eyes and minds have to be open to see areas of school and the curriculum that are not diverse friendly, and teachers have to try to change those unfriendly obstacles to learning.

Fourth, once teachers have made a personal commitment to be more diverse and to embrace diversity, then the world opens up for all students. Teachers can then see gaps in the curriculum, gaps in the way teachers talk to students, gaps in the assumptions teachers have about students, gaps in knowledge of different cultures, gaps in expectations for students, and gaps in understanding of what different students need to be successful. Then, of course, once educators know where the gaps are, something has to be done to close those gaps.

This is an exciting time in education because the art of teaching has an opportunity to return to school. Teachers can become the creative and caring people who first came into the field of education. Teachers can become transformers of lives for their students. Instead of holding students accountable, teachers can inspire their students to make the world a better place.

Complex Independent and Group Projects

Caine (2018), Johnson and Johnson (2009), Sousa (2017), and the authors of this book advocate for immersing students in complex projects. Students should complete complex work both individually and in small groups. It is essential that students do the difficult work of being part of a team that is responsible to each other to accomplish important and complex tasks. Students have to work with other people on a regular basis to build their critical-thinking and social skills. They also have to work individually to build their independence skills.

Positive Contributing Teammates

When students work in groups on important projects, they have to be taught how to consider two important elements of being a part of a team: (1) the goals of the work (academic goals) and (2) the relationships between and among team members (social goals). There are jobs that must be accomplished, and each member of the group must perform their job for the group to be effective. Each member has to be individually accountable for their work. Teams work best when they are interdependent—understand that they need each other to accomplish the task at hand.

This combination of individual accountability and group interdependence is important to prepare students for their lives after graduation. In the real world, important work usually gets accomplished through teamwork. Obviously, work in families depends on the ability of people to build strong relationships and work together as a unit. Learning the negotiation skills, collaborative skills, the ability to hold oneself accountable, and to be accountable to and for others prepares students for their future lives.

One way to visualize this process is through what Johnson and Johnson (2009) call the Basic Elements of Formal Cooperative Learning. Table 6.5 displays the basic elements with a short definition for each element. When developing, implementing, and assessing lessons, teachers can use these elements to assist them in assessing what went well and what needs improvement in small group work.

Table 6.5 Cooperative Learning Basic Elements

Element	Definition
Positive interdependence	Set up the process so students believe they need each other to successfully learn the material and complete the project
Individual accountability	Each individual is responsible to accomplish their piece of the work, learn the material, and help the group accomplish the task at hand
Promotive interaction	Students learn and employ behaviors that help the group and the individuals in progress personally, socially, and academically
Social/small group skills	Skills that promote the development of the group (e.g., sharing, negotiating, discussing, and encouraging)
Active processing	Students assess themselves and group members socially and academically, describing what worked well, what needs improvement, and a plan for improvement

Sources: Johnson and Johnson (2009) and Laurin-Fitzgerald and Fitzgerald (2016).

Teachers also can develop experiences for students to learn and develop skills in each of the elements. For example, teachers might teach specific promotive skills, such as encouragement, inclusionary actions, or active listening. When teaching students these concepts and skills, it is important to remember to help students progress through the skill development processes: (1) awareness, (2) initial skill-building, (3) guided skill-building, (4) independent practice, and (5) independent competence. As students become proficient in one skill, it is time to begin the process with the next skill.

Individual Ownership

Whether the project is an independent or a group project, the system should be developed so students are taking more and more responsibility for their work. Students should learn at a young age how to develop topics for their projects. At the beginning, students could be given choices of topics from a list provided by the teacher. The list could be as short as two items for young students. Students should learn how to do different kinds of projects (e.g., research, experiments, interviews, documentaries, proposals, portfolios, performances).

When students have had some experience, they should be offered the ability to develop their goals, topics, and products. The teacher moves more and more toward being a guide and/or mentor to the students, as students develop more and more independence. Experiences have shown that some teachers struggle with these kinds of changes in the power dynamic in their classes. Some feel out of control and this can be frightening.

One key is to move students along the continuum from dependent to independent learner at an appropriate pace. That is, do not give the students more than they can handle, and do not keep them back when they are ready to move ahead. The same ideas seem true for teachers—move at a pace that is comfortable for you.

Complexity

A key aspect of these projects must be their complexity. It is usually a good idea to develop projects that have different levels of complexity in which students display what they know and can do. Within the projects, students should (1) show they know and understand the basic elements of their learning (e.g., vocabulary, rules, formulas); (2) be able to apply and analyze a situation employing the knowledge, tools, or skills being learned; (3) use the knowledge, tools, and skills to synthesize previous learning with new learning to evaluate, synthesize ideas and skills, and create solutions for a complex issue or set of questions.

Conclusion

Remember, the object of most of learning is independent learning. Almost everything students learn should help them to become more independent learners and active citizens. Explicit teaching is important. Following the five-step process will help teachers assist students to become more and more independent: (1) awareness, (2) initial skill-building, (3) guided skill-building, (4) independent practice, and (5) independent competence. In general terms, it might help to think of this process as (a) engage, (b) introduce, (c) I do, (d) we do, and (e) you do. The goal, of course, is to get every student to the independent *you do* stage.

Pursue Interests, Talents, and Passions

Often in school, teachers will say something like, "Many of my students do not seem to have big interests or passions." So, how can they integrate student interest into teaching when they do not exist in so many students? This is a very legitimate issue, but in so many cases it is not the fault of the students that they appear to not have passions or strong interests, because they have never had opportunities to explore life in order to begin to develop interests or passions. One goal of student-centered teaching and learning is to help students at least begin to develop their individual interests.

One of the huge benefits of bringing diversity of people, ideas, art forms, career examples, and experiences into the classroom (or the classroom into the community) is that it opens more of the world to students. In this age of technology, teachers have so many more options to expose students to the world. Naturally, teachers cannot expose students to everything, but that is a poor excuse to not expose students to anything. Integrating the world into classroom lessons not only sparks more interest in students, but it also opens students to possibilities. Thus, the first step in helping students develop their interests is to expose them to as many diverse experiences as possible.

How can schools meet the goal of helping students to be career ready? Expose them to a diversity of careers. Too many schools and teachers believe that career and college ready really means college ready. That assumption is just false thinking. As a matter of fact, people like Wagner (2014) and Robinson (2017) tell us that many college graduates are ill-prepared for any career. Amanda Bastoni (chapter 4) describes how CTE programs actually do prepare their students for careers. Comprehensive high schools would do well to learn from their CTE colleagues.

Throughout their academic journeys, as students pursue their projects, they should experience a diverse range of topics, careers, people, lifestyles, art forms, and points of view. For example, when one observes student drawings on the wall of classrooms, are they all the same, or, are they displaying diverse views of the world? Even if the goal is to help students draw within the lines, why, in some classes, are all of the lines the same? If students are drawing within people lines, why cannot the people be from a diversity of communities and careers? Should not first graders ask their teachers questions like: "What is a welder?" "Who was Mother Teresa?"

In order to develop talents, students must be actively engaged in doing a variety of activities. How can students know if they have talent, if they never attempt to do a multitude of activities requiring a variety of experiences and skills? Students should be exposed to as many different kinds of activities as possible, so they can try their hands at different kinds of skills (e.g., sing; dance; act; build; run; draw; paint; speak publicly; write poetry; read about the world; develop experiments; or design clothing, houses, cars, and rockets).

Unlike what many believe, for most people, talent is developed through effort, rehearsal, and practice. Dweck (2016) tells us that many of the greatest artists, actors, designers, and the like did not start out being great. What they did was to find an interest, and they developed it through hard work and perseverance. Additionally, being interested in one thing often leads people to find related interests. How many journalists out there started with an interest (e.g., history, sports, politics, or art) and later found they also had an interest in talking and writing about their first interest?

One very important assumption for teachers at every level of education must be that it is every teacher's job to help their students find and pursue their interests, talents, and passions. If teachers see their teaching as opportunities to also expose their children to diverse ideas, people, and careers, then they will think about diversity in most of what they do. If, on the other hand, teachers believe they only have to teach (fill in the subject), so their students will pass the common exams, then they will deprive their students of opportunities to search out, find, and develop their interests, talents, and passions.

The notion that students will somehow find and develop their interests, talents, and passions through some process like osmosis is ridiculous. Schools must help students by exposing them to as much as possible, and by allowing students to explore as much as possible. Teachers must have the courage to move into areas about which they know nothing, so they can help their students discover new ideas and skills. Teachers do not have to know everything; teachers need to know how to find out what they and their students want and need to know.

If teachers limit students by exposing them only to what the teacher knows, then students are being deprived of untold opportunities. Think of how much more fun teaching will be if teachers are learning from and with students on a regular basis. The opportunities for the art of teaching are right there in the hearts and minds of our students. It is time for teachers to take back education for the sake of students.

Personalized Learning

Everything discussed in this chapter leads to the final discussion point, learning should be personalized for every student. Teachers understand all students are individuals who have had different life experiences; live in different socioeconomic circumstances (SES); learn in different ways; have developed differently and been exposed to different degrees of learning; have different emotional states, interests, and talents; and have developed different need profiles. This is common knowledge, so why then do so many schools continue to act as if every student is the same, learns in one way, should be assessed in a single way, and will develop their interests in spite of school instead of with the help of school?

If someone came to a school board with a proposal that stated the new school will ignore differences in development, learning processes, SES, cultures, emotional needs, and special education needs, that person would be thrown out of the meeting. In schools though, all too often, many of those differences are ignored. School has become more about conformity than it is about personal and group development. This has to change, if we really care about the future of our students.

In a student-centered educational process, all of the differences and similarities of students would be taken into important consideration when developing student programs. The point is to develop each individual to meet their potential. That cannot be accomplished under the current model. Educators must learn to change assumptions about students and schooling and must learn how to implement new roles as mentors, guides, and student advocates.

The time is at hand when teachers and principals can actually take back education from the politicians and businesspeople. If teachers fail to act now, this opportunity will pass and, as Ruthann Petruno-Goguen (chapter 5) would say, *status quo* will win the day. That would be a tragedy for teachers and students.

It has been said that the definition of insanity is continuing to do the same things and expecting different results. It appears in many ways that education is insane. As in casinos, where the house always wins, politicians and many educational leaders have continued to *double down* on accountability. The major problem is that education is betting on the lives of real students, not betting chips, and our teachers and students are losing.

Students, by the millions, are being left broken because of our insanity. From a big picture perspective, politicians refuse to address poverty; schools continue to exhibit institutional racism, sexism, and cultural bias; curriculum specialists ignore the diversity of our nation and the world; and teaching techniques continue to stress curriculum goals set by groups of adults who each believe their specialty area is a discrete predetermined set of information and concepts that every students should learn in the same way.

Many schools continue to use *teacher-proof* curriculum programs that tell teachers how to teach, when to teach, and how to pace the curriculum so that every student is literally on the same page, on the same day, at the same minute. It is insane. If educators continue to follow this process, which at best is outdated, and at its worst is purposefully making the rich richer, the poor poorer, and the people in the middle disenfranchised, our students will be ill-prepared for their lives after graduation.

Effective education is not about conformity, it is about creativity; it is not about accountability, it is about inspiration; it is not about test results, it is about performance in the real world; it is not about narrow thinking, it is about diversity. At its core, education is about generating differently educated people who will be positive, productive, and active citizens who understand there is a balance between individual rights and freedoms and the collective welfare of all citizens.

Here is our list of what to work on to reach personalized learning. Teachers should:

1. create safe and caring environments;
2. scaffold for all students who need assistance;
3. maintain high standards for all students;
4. universally design the curriculum for all students;

5. create positive relationships between the teacher and the students and between and among all students;
6. meet the emotional, intellectual, physical, and social needs of all students;
7. ensure every student has a voice;
8. create equity for all students;
9. celebrate diversity; and
10. give progressively more authority and responsibility for learning to the students.

Everything discussed in this book should result in the items in this list being brought to life.

To help students reach their potential, teachers must work with students to develop personal goals for the short term and for the long term. There are a multitude of ways that students could and should demonstrate their understandings, knowledge, and skills. State or national competencies should not be addressed by narrowing the curriculum and making every student display what they have learned by common assessments. Teachers should personalize assessments to be in line with student goals and dreams. During their early years in school, students should be taught how to set goals for themselves, how to self-assess their progress, how to take and use teacher feedback, and how to develop as independent learners.

Voice and choice are vital elements to any student's education. In the long run, the ability to independently think; understand different ideas, people, and cultures; and to adapt to a changing society will determine the future of the world. Everything discussed in this chapter is a different perspective on this same theme. The goal is to generate intelligent, curious, creative, and critically thinking citizens who will work hard to improve our world.

SUPERVISING TEACHERS

One of the most important ways for teachers to grow is to have supervisors who understand teachers and teaching and who see teacher growth as an integral part of their jobs. Superintendents set the environment for their districts, and how they work with principals and teachers matters. If superintendents do not help principals and other administrators to grow, then the district will remain *status quo*. One very important aspect of the job of an administrator is to challenge that *status quo* and to change it when necessary. The *status quo* simply must be transformed or schools will continue to fail their students.

Principals must believe that it is important to help teachers grow. If administrators want teachers to be student-centered, then principals must be student-centered, and they must be teacher-centered. It is cute to say, "It is all about the students," but if principals are not also teacher-centered they either are lying or are fooling themselves. A principal cannot really be student-centered unless they are also teacher-centered. Not only must principals challenge the *status quo*, but they must also help teachers do the same. Principals must supervise teachers as professional colleagues, and work with teachers to assist them in their professional growth.

First, administration (superintendent and all other administrators) must be on the same page that education must be student-centered. This means the vision and the mission of the district and every school in the district has to be student-centered. If the vision and mission statements are not student-centered, they need changing. In order to be student-centered, the vision and mission of the administration must also be teacher-centered. Those vision and mission statements must be aligned with these notions.

Second, the professional development programs in the district and the schools must be adequately funded so that teacher training is fully supported. Districts have to put their money where their mouths are. If districts and schools do not support the professional development of their teachers, then all the rest is a smoke screen. It is rather simple; if districts and schools do not support professional development, then little will change. Student-centered teaching requires radically different roles for teachers and principals, and without systematic and strategic training it will not happen.

Third, how superintendents assess and supervise principals, and how principals assess and supervise teachers must be principal-centered and teacher-centered, respectively, with an eye on student-centered teaching. For example, two critical questions must be answered: (1) *How do principals assess the needs of their teachers?* (2) *How do principals ask teachers to assess their own needs?* Both of these questions have to be related to student-centered teaching. Principals must ask the same kinds of questions for teachers: (1) *How do teachers assess the needs of their students?* (2) *How do teachers get students to assess their own needs?* Naturally, the next question is something like: *What do principals/teachers do with the information they gather?*

The process must ensure that principals and teachers can implement the following:

1. create safe and caring environments;
2. proactively scaffold for all students who need assistance;
3. maintain high standards for all students;
4. universally design the curriculum for all students;
5. create positive relationships between the teacher and the students and between and among all students;

6. meet the emotional, intellectual, physical, and social needs of all students;
7. ensure every student has a voice;
8. create equity for all students;
9. celebrate diversity; and
10. give progressively more authority and responsibility for learning to the students.

Principals and teachers should have a format to self-assess and be assessed on the ten elements of student-centered teaching listed here. Naturally, these are suggestions, and district should develop their own list and forms. The important point is that district and school leaders must understand student-centered teaching and learning, so they can supervise their colleagues appropriately.

With that in mind, questions like the following might be added to an existing template used to assess teacher plans for teaching important units:

1. What techniques will be used to ensure this unit is student-centered?
2. How will students be assisted to move along the continuum from dependence to independence as learners?
3. How is student choice employed in this unit?
4. What scaffolds are proactively in place to ensure all students can be successful (considering they put forth honest efforts)?
5. What universally designed strategies will be employed in this unit?
6. How will feedback be gathered from students to help adapt lessons during the unit?
7. What forms of feedback will be used to help students adapt their efforts during this unit?
8. How will students use their strengths to display what they have learned and can do with their learning?
9. How will students employ their interests, talents, or passions in this unit?

Then, based on the self-assessments, co-assessments, and supervisor assessments, professional development plans have to be developed and implemented. It might make sense to create a three-year plan with yearly goals. It is vital that the district and school support these plans so they actually can be fully implemented.

Administrators and teachers should work together to creatively and effectively develop professional development within the district and in individual schools. For example, a district might implement and financially support a summer professional development program for principals and teachers. There are many ways to do the work, and, if administration and teachers work together cooperatively, every district has enough brainpower and talent to accomplish these goals.

Fourth, schools and districts should create hiring practices that ensure new teachers are recruited who have the mentality to be student-centered teachers. During interviews it should be abundantly obvious that teachers must be student-centered in order to work in the district or school. Prior to being hired, new teachers should generate their self-assessment and their first three-year plan. Those documents should be required prior to signing their first contract. They should also know that the district and school are serious about student-centered teaching, and their future employment in the district is dependent on their enthusiastic buy-in to student-centered teaching (Pink, 2006; Zhao, 2012).

Finally, it is vital that administrators support and assist their teachers in this process. They must get to know their teachers in the same way they want teachers to get to know their students. Administrators should support teachers in the same way they want teachers to support their students. They should develop professional growth in a personalized way, just as they want teachers to personalize learning for their students. Administrators must walk the talk, just as they want teachers to do for their students.

CONCLUSIONS

The future of the world is dependent on how well we educate our students. If we choose to maintain the *status quo*, the future could be disastrous. The system is outdated, and it is time to transform education so that it is organized to help all students become independent learners, critical thinkers, and well-educated people who understand how to balance their individual needs and rights with the collective good. Students have to be skilled to be both independent and interdependent. They will have to be technologically savvy, creative, and persistent in their efforts to make the world a better place.

Teachers and administrators must understand the future expectations and become proficient in helping every student to become a successful learner. We cannot afford less. It is a complex and difficult job, but we are educators, and we can make it work. Teachers and administrators have all of the potential necessary to transform education. Educators need support to transform schools, and, if that happens, it will change the face of education. If communities and educators work together cooperatively, it will unleash the power of learning and the potential of all students. What an exciting time to be a teacher!

References

Abeles, V., & Congdon, J. (Directors). (2010). *Race to nowhere* [Motion picture]. United States: Reel Link Films.

Abeles, V., & Rubenstein, G. (2016). *Beyond measure: Rescuing an overscheduled, overtested, underestimated generation.* New York: Simon & Schuster Paperbacks.

ACT. (2016). The condition of STEM 2016. Retrieved from http://www.act.org/content/dam/act/unsecured/documents/STEM2016_52_National.pdf.

Adelman, C. (2004). *Principal indicators of student academic histories in postsecondary education, 1972–2000.* Washington, DC: U.S. Department of Education, Institute of Education Sciences.

Aiken, L. R. (1976). Update on attitudes and other affective variables in learning mathematics. *Review of Educational Research, 46*(2), 293–311. doi:10.2307/1170042.

Aisch, G., Buchanan, L., Cox, A., & Quealy, K. (2017, January 18). Some colleges have more students from the top 1 percent than the bottom 60. Find yours. *New York Times.* Retrieved from https://www.nytimes.com/interactive/2017/01/18/upshot/some-colleges-have-more-students-from-the-top-1-percent-than-the-bottom-60.html.

Aliaga, M., Cobb, G., Cuff, C., Garfield, J., Gould, R., Lock, R., . . . & Witmer, J. (2005). *Guidelines for assessment and instruction in statistical education (GAISE): College report.* Alexandria, VA: American Statistical Association.

American Mathematical Association of Two-Year Colleges. (1995). *Crossroads in mathematics—Standards for introductory college mathematics before calculus.* Author. Retrieved from http://www.imacc.org/standards/.

American Mathematical Association of Two-Year Colleges. (2006). *Beyond crossroads—Implementing mathematics standards in the first two years of college.* Author. Retrieved from http://beyondcrossroads.matyc.org/.

American Statistical Association. (2005). *Guidelines for assessment and instruction in statistical education (GAISE): College report.* Alexandria, VA: American Statistical Association.

Andrusiak, R. A. (2018). *Real-time classroom factors impacting middle-school students' attitudes toward mathematics* (Doctoral Dissertation). Retrieved from ProQuest Dissertations and Theses Database (ProQuest No: 10933664).

Aoun, J. E. (2017). *Robot-proof: Higher education in the age of artificial intelligence* [Kindle Edition]. Retrieved from Amazon.com. Cambridge, MA: The MIT Press.

Armstrong, T. (2012). *Neurodiversity in the classroom: Strength-based strategies.* Alexandria, VA: Association of Supervision and Curriculum Development.

Attewell, P., Lavin, D., Domina, T., & Levey, T. (2006). New evidence on college remediation. *The Journal of Higher Education, 77*(5), 886–924. doi:10.1080/00221546.2006.11778948.

Belbase, S. (2013). Images, anxieties, and attitudes toward mathematics. *International Journal of Education in Mathematics, Science and Technology, 1*(4), 230–237.

Black, P., Harrison, C., Lee, C., Marshall, B., & Wiliam, D. (2003). *Assessment for learning: Putting it into practice.* Berkshire, UK: Open University Press.

Blad, E. (2017, February 9). More than half of students "engaged" in school, says poll. Retrieved from http://www.edweek.org/ew/articles/2014/04/09/28gallup.h33.html.

Bloom, B. (1956). *Taxonomy of educational objectives book 1: Cognitive domain.* (2nd Ed.). New York: Longman.

Borman, G. D., Hewes, G. M., Overman, L. T., & Brown, S. (2002). *Comprehensive school reform and student achievement: A meta-analysis.* (Rep.). Retrieved from http://nec.gmilcs.org/login?url=http://search.ebscohost.com/login.aspx?direct=true&AuthType=cookie,ip,url,cpid&custid=danforth&db=eric&AN=ED472569&site=ehost-live&scope=site.

Bramante, F., & Colby, R. (2012). *Off the clock: Moving education from time to competency.* Thousand Oaks, CA: Corwin.

Brown, B. (2017). *Braving the wilderness: The quest for true belonging and the courage to stand alone.* New York: Random House.

Bruner, J. S. (1961). The act of discovery. *Harvard Educational Review, 31*(1): 21–32.

Business Higher Education Forum (2011, November). *Meeting the STEM workforce challenge: Leveraging higher education's untapped potential to prepare tomorrow's STEM workforce* (Policy brief). Retrieved from http://eric.ed.gov/?id=ED527257.

Caine, G. (2018). Making connections between e-learning and natural learning. In C. Fitzgerald, S. Laurian-Fitzgerald, & C. Popa (eds.). *Handbook of research on student-centered strategies in online adult learning environments.* Hershey, PA: IGI Global.

Caine, R. N., & Caine, G. (2011). *Natural learning for a connected world.* New York, NY: Teachers College Press.

Caine, R. N., Caine, G., McClintic, C. L., & Klimek, K. L. (2016). *12 brain/mind learning principles in action: Teach for the development of higher-order thinking and executive function.* (3rd Ed.). Thousand Oaks, CA: Corwin.

Carnevale, A. P., Hanson, A. R., & Fasules, M. (2018, September 19). *"Career ready" out of high school? Why the nation needs to let go of that myth.* Retrieved from http://theconversation.com/career-ready-out-of-high-school-why-the-nation-needs-to-let-go-of-that-myth-88288.

Cass, O. (2018, December 10). *The misguided priorities of our educational system.* Retrieved from https://www.nytimes.com/2018/12/10/opinion/college-vocational-education-students.html.

CAST. (2018). *Universal design for learning guidelines, version 2.2.* Retrieved from http://udlguidelines.cast.org.

Choi, N., & Chang, M. (2011, January 1). Interplay among school climate, gender, attitude toward mathematics, and mathematics performance of middle school students. *Middle Grades Research Journal, 6*(1), 15–28.

Christensen, C.M., Horn, M.B., & Johnson, C.W. (2011). *Disrupting class: How disruptive innovation will change the way the world learns.* New York: McGraw-Hill.

Coalition of Essential Schools. (n.d.). *Student-centered teaching and learning.* Retrieved from http://essentialschools.org/benchmarks/student-centered-teaching-and-learning/.

Complete College America. (2016a). *Corequisite remediation* [PowerPoint Slides]. Retrieved from http://completecollege.org/wp-content/uploads/2015/10/Coreq-SuccessatScale.pptx.

Complete College America. (2016b). *Corequisite remediation: Spanning the completion divide.* Washington, DC: Author. Retrieved from http://completecollege.org/spanningthedivide/.

Complete College America. (2017). *Corequisite remediation: New Hampshire CCA data snapshot.* Indianapolis, IN: Author.

Connley, C. (2018). *Mike Rowe of dirty jobs says follow your passion is bad advice—Here's what to do instead.* Retrieved from https://www.cnbc.com/2018/12/06/mike-rowe-of-dirty-jobs-says-follow-opportunity-not-passion.html.

Costa, A. L., & Kallick, B. (2008). *Learning and leading with habits of mind: 16 essential characteristics for success.* Alexandria, VA: Association for Supervision and Curriculum Development.

Couros, G. (2015). *The innovator's mindset: Empower learning, unleash talent, and lead a culture of creativity.* San Diego, CA: Dave Burgess Consulting.

Csikszentmihalyi, M. (1990; 2008). *Flow: The psychology of optimal experience.* New York: Harper Perennial Modern Classics.

Cullinane, J., & Treisman, P. U. (2010). *Improving developmental mathematics education in two-year colleges: A prospectus and early progress report on the Statway Initiative.* New York: National Center for Post-secondary Research.

Cushing, H. A. (1904). *The writings of Samuel Adams.* New York: G.P. Putnam's Sons. Retrieved from https://www.conservapedia.com/Samuel_Adams_to_James_Warren_(February_12,_1779).

Davidson, C. N. (2017). *The new education: How to revolutionize the university to prepare students for a world in flux.* New York: Basic Books.

Deming, D. J. (2017). *The value of soft skills in the labor market.* Retrieved from https://www.nber.org/reporter/2017number4/deming.html.

Dewey, J. (1910). *How we think.* Boston, MA: D.C. Heath Publishers.

Diera, C. (2016, August). Democratic possibilities for student voice within schools undergoing reform: A student counterpublic case study. *Journal for Critical Education Policy Studies (JCEPS)*, *14*(2), 217–235. Retrieved from Education Research Complete.

DiMartino, J., & Clarke, J. H. (2008). *Personalizing the high school experience for each student*. Alexandria, VA: Association for Supervision and Curriculum Development.

Di Martino, P., & Zan, R. (2003, July). *What does "positive" attitude really mean?* Paper presented at International Group for the Psychology of Mathematics Education, Honolulu, HI.

Di Martino, P., & Zan, R. (2010, February). Me and maths: Towards a definition of attitude grounded on students' narratives. *Journal of Mathematics Teacher Education*, *13*(1), 27–48. doi:10.1007/s10857-009-9134-z.

DiMartino, J., Wolk, D., & Curtis, P. (2010). *The personalized high school: Making learning count for adolescents*. San Francisco, CA: Jossey-Bass.

Dintersmith, T. (2018). *What school could be: Insights and inspiration from teachers across America*. Princeton, NJ: Princeton University Press.

Dougherty, M. S. (2016). *Career and technical education in high school: Does it improve student outcomes*. Washington, DC: Thomas B. Fordham Institute.

Duckworth, A. (2016). *Grit: The power of passion and perseverance*. New York: Scribner.

Dweck, C. S. (2016). *Mindset: The new psychology of success*. New York: Balantine Books.

Eleftherios, K., & Theodosius, Z. (2007). Students' beliefs and attitude about studying and learning mathematics. In J. H. Woo, H. C. Lew, K. S. Park, & D. Y. Seo (eds.). *Proceedings of the 31st conference on the international group for the psychology of mathematics education*, Vol. 3 (pp. 97–104). Seoul: Psychology of Mathematics Education.

Elmore, R. F. (2007). *School reform from the inside out: Policy, practice, and performance*. Cambridge, MA: Harvard Education Press.

Epsilon Data Management, LLC. (2018, January). *New Epsilon research indicates 80% of consumers are more likely to make a purchase when brands offer personalized experiences*. Retrieved from https://us.epsilon.com/pressroom/new-epsilon-research-indicates-80-of-consumers-are-more-likely-to-make-a-purchase-when-brands-offer-personalized-experiences.

Evers, J., & Kneyber, R. (eds.). (2016). *Flip the system: Changing education from the ground up*. New York: Routledge.

Falzon, K. (2017, April 20). *Do not underestimate the importance of career technical education*. Retrieved from https://workingnation.com/not-underestimate-importance-career-technical-education/.

Fitzgerald, C. (2003). *Inner balance: The pathway to positive relationships*. New London, NH: Carlton Fitzgerald.

Fitzgerald, C., & Johnson, K. (2013). A study of the emotional climate in the classroom. *The New Hampshire Journal of Education*, *XVI* (Spring), 69–73.

Fitzgerald, C., & Laurian, S. (2013). Caring our way to more effective learning. *Procedia-Social and Behavioral Sciences*, *76*(2013), 341–345. Available online at www.sciencedirect.com.

The Foundation and Center for Critical Thinking. (2017). *Strategy list: 35 dimensions of critical thought*. Retrieved from http://www.criticalthinking.org/pages/strategy-list-35-dimensions-of-critical-thought/466.

Frankl, V. I. (2006). *Man's search for meaning*. Boston, MA: Beacon Press.

Fullan, M., Hargreaves, A., & Rincon-Gallardo, S. (2015). Professional capital as accountability. *Education Policy Analysis Archives*, 23(15). doi:10.14507/epaa.v23.1998.

Fullan, M., & Langworthy, M. (2013). *Towards a new end: New pedagogies for deep learning*. Seattle, WA: Collaborative Impact.

Fullan, M., & Langworthy, M. (2014). *A rich seam: How new pedagogies find deep learning*. London, UK: Pearson.

GAISE College Report ASA Revision Committee. (2016). *Guidelines for assessment and instruction in statistics education college report 2016*. Retrieved from http://www.amstat.org/education/gaise.

Gall, M. D., Gall, J. P., & Borg, W. R. (2007). *Educational research: An introduction*. (8th Ed.). Boston, MA: Pearson.

Gallup, Inc. (2017). *The Gallup 2017 superintendent survey of K–12 school district superintendents*. Retrieved from https://news.gallup.com/reports/217103/gallup-k-12-superintendent-report-201708.aspx.

Ganter, S.L., & Haver, W.E. (eds.). (2011). Partner discipline recommendations for introductory college mathematics and the implications for college algebra. *Mathematical Association of America*. Retrieved from https://www.maa.org/sites/default/files/pdf/CUPM/crafty/introreport.pdf.

Garcia, E., & Weiss, E. (2019). *The teacher shortage is real, large and growing, and worse than we thought*. Retrieved from https://www.epi.org/files/pdf/163651.pdf.

Gardner, H. (1983; 2011). *Frames of mind: The theory of multiple intelligences*. New York: Basic Books.

George, P. S., & Florida Educational Research and Development Council. (1975). Ten years of open space schools; A review of the research. *Research Bulletin* (Vol. 9). Retrieved from http://nec.gmilcs.org/login?url=http://search.ebscohost.com/login.aspx?direct=true&AuthType=cookie,ip,url,cpid&custid=danforth&db=eric&AN=ED110431&site=ehost-live&scope=site.

Gladwell, M. (2008). *Outliers: The story of success*. New York: Little, Brown and Co.

Gladwell, M. (2016, June 30). *The big man can't shoot with Malcolm Gladwell | E3 /S1: Revisionist History Podcast* (Transcript). Retrieved from https://blog.simonsays.ai/the-big-man-cant-shoot-with-malcolm-gladwell-e3-s1-revisionist-history-podcast-transcript-1b87d82c2546.

Glasser, W. (1998). *Choice theory: A new psychology of personal freedom*. New York: HarperCollins.

Glasser, W. (2006). *Every student can succeed: Finally a book that explains how to reach and teach every student in your school*. Mosheim, TN: Black Forest Press.

Goldin, G. A., Hannula, M. S., Heyd-Metzuyanim, E. H., Jansen, A., Kaasila, R., Lutovac, S., & Zhang, Q. (2016). *Attitudes, beliefs, motivation and identity in mathematics education: An overview of the field and future directions* [eBook version]. doi: 10.1007/978-3-319-32811-9.

Goudas, A. M. (2017, March). *The corequisite reform movement: An education bait and switch*. Retrieved from http://communitycollegedata.com/articles/the-corequisite-reform-movement/.

Graf, N. (2018). *A Majority of U.S. Teens fear a shooting could happen at their school, and most parents share their concerns*. Retrieved from https://www.pewresearch.org/fact-tank/2018/04/18/a-majority-of-u-s-teens-fear-a-shooting-could-happen-at-their-school-and-most-parents-share-their-concern/.

Hammond, Z. L. (2015). *Culturally responsive teaching and the brain: Promoting authentic engagement and rigor among culturally and linguistically diverse students*. Thousand Oaks, CA: Corwin.

Hammond, Z. L., & Jackson, Y. (2015). *Culturally responsive teaching and the brain: Promoting authentic engagement and rigor among culturally and linguistically diverse students*. Thousand Oaks, CA: Corwin.

Hattie, J. (2009). *Visible learning: A synthesis of over 800 meta-analyses relating to achievement*. London, UK: Routledge.

Hattie, J. (2012). *Visible learning for teachers: Maximizing impact on learning*. London, UK: Routledge.

Hargreaves, A., & Fullan, M. (2012). *Professional capital: Transforming teaching in every school*. New York: Teachers College Press.

Hargreaves, A., & Goodson, I. (2006). Educational change over time? The sustainability and nonsustainability of three decades of secondary school change and continuity. *Educational Administration Quarterly*, *42*(1), 3–41. doi:10.1177/0013161x05277975.

Horn, R. A. (2002). *Understanding educational reform: A reference handbook. Contemporary education issues*. Santa Barbara, CA: ABC-CLIO, Inc.

Idil, F. H., Narli, S., & Aksoy, E. (2016, January 1). Using data mining techniques: Examination of the middle school students' attitude towards mathematics in the context of some variables. *International Journal of Education in Mathematics, Science and Technology*, *4*(3), 210–228.

Jeffrey, P. T. (2019). *Federal report: 220,300 public school teachers physically attacked by students*. Retrieved from https://www.cnsnews.com/news/article/terence-p-jeffrey/federal-report-220300-public-school-teachers-physically-attacked.

Jenkins, D., & Fink, J. (2018, September 4). *New insights for guided pathways reforms from research on community college student momentum* [Web blog post]. Retrieved from https://ccrc.tc.columbia.edu/blog/new-insights-for-guided-pathways-reforms.html.

Jennings, P. A. (2019). *The trauma-sensitive classroom: Building resilience with compassionate teaching* [Kindle Edition]. New York: W. W. Norton & Company.

Jensen, E. (2009). *Teaching with poverty in mind: What being poor does to kids' brains and what schools can do about it*. Alexandria, VA: Association for Supervision and Curriculum Development.

Jimenez, L., Sargrad, S., Morales, J., & Thompson, M. (2016, September 28). Remedial education: The cost of catching up. *Center for American Progress*. Retrieved from https://www.americanprogress.org/issues/education-k-12/reports/2016/09/28/144000/remedial-education/.

Johnson, D. W., & Johnson, R. T. (2009). *Joining together: Group theory and group skills* (10th ed.). Boston, MA: Allyn & Bacon.

Johnson, D. W., & Johnson, R. T. (2013). The impact of cooperative, competitive, and individualistic learning environments on achievement. In J. Hattie, & E. Anderman (eds.). *International handbook of student achievement* (pp. 372–74). New York, NY: Routledge.

Juliani, A. J. (2015). *Inquiry and innovation in the classroom: Using 20% time, genius hour, and PBL to drive student success.* New York: Routledge.

Kahlenberg, D. R., & Potter, H. (2014). *Why teacher voice matters.* Retrieved from https://files.eric.ed.gov/fulltext/EJ1049443.pdf.

Kane, M., Berryman, S., Goslin, D., & Meltzer, A. (1990). *Identifying and describing the skills required by work. The Secretary's Commission on achieving necessary skills. Employment and Training Administration.* Washington, DC: U.S. Department of Labor.

Kansky, R. (2008). RSS #83: The extent and cost of postsecondary remediation. *National Council of Supervisors of Mathematics.* Retrieved from http://ncsmonline.org/OtherResources/rss.html.

King, M. L., Jr. (1947). The purpose of education. *Maroon tiger.* (January–February 1947). Retrieved from http://okra.stanford.edu/transcription/document_images/Vol01Scans/123_Jan-Feb1947_The%20Purpose%20of%20Education.pdf.

Kolb, D. A. (1984). *Experiential learning.* Englewood Cliffs, NJ: Prentice Hall, Inc.

Kraft, M. A. (2010). From ringmaster to conductor: 10 simple techniques can turn an unruly class into a productive one. *Phi Delta Kappan, 91*(7), 44–47.

Kraus & Boss. (2013). *Thinking through project-based learning: Guiding deeper inquiry.* (1st Ed.). Thousand Oaks, CA: Corwin Press.

Kreisman, D., & Stange, K. (2019). Depth over breadth. *Education Next, 19*(4). Retrieved from https://www.educationnext.org/depth-over-breadth-value-vocational-education-u-s-high-schools/.

Larson, R., & Csikszentmihalyi, M. (1983). The experience sampling method. In H. G. Reis (ed.). *Naturalistic approaches to studying social instruction* (pp. 42–56). San Francisco, CA: Jossey-Bass.

Laurian-Fitzgerald, S., & Fitzgerald, C. (2016). Cooperative learning and mindset with young students. *Revista STUDIA UBB PSYCHOL.-PAED., LXI*(1), 63–82, Cluj-Napoca.

Laurian-Fitzgerald, S., & Fitzgerald, C. (2018). Student-centered learning in undergraduate preservice teachers. *The European proceedings of social & behavioural sciences.* Presented at EDU WORLD 2018 The 8th International Conference.

Laurian-Fitzgerald, S., Popa, C., & Fitzgerald, C. J. (2015). The race to reach standards: Are we forgetting about our students? *Romanian Journal of School Psychology, 8*(16), 90–96.

Lawson, E. (2017, September 21). *New research: Diversity + inclusion = better decision making at work.* Retrieved from https://www.forbes.com/sites/eriklarson/2017/09/21/new-research-diversity-inclusion-better-decision-making-at-work/#3fe520784cbf.

Lea, S. J., Stephenson, D., & Troy, J. (2003). Higher education students' attitudes to student-centered learning: Beyond "educational bulimia." *Studies in Higher Education, 28*(3), 321–334.

Lee, K. F. (2018). *2019–09–04-Kai-Fu Lee + future of AI*. Retrieved from https://www.youtube.com/watch?v=tUX4ctv-WBo.

Lee, K. F. (2019). *AI superpowers: China, silicon valley, and the new world order*. New York: Houghton Mifflin Harcourt Publishing Company.

Logue, A. W. (2018, July 17). *The extensive evidence of co-requisite remediation's effectiveness*. Retrieved from https://www.insidehighered.com/views/2018/07/17/data-already-tell-us-how-effective-co-requisite-education-opinion.

Logue, A. W., Watanabe-Rose, M., & Douglas, D. (2016). Should students assessed as needing remedial mathematics take college-level quantitative courses instead? A randomized controlled trial. *Educational Evaluation and Policy Analysis*, *38*(3), 578–598. doi:10.3102/0162373716649056.

Loveless, T. (2017, March). How well are American students learning? *The 2017 Brown Center Report on American Education*, *3*(6). Retrieved from https://www.brookings.edu/wp-content/uploads/2017/03/2017-brown-center-report-on-american-education.pdf.

The MacDowell Colony. (n.d.). *Frequently asked questions*. Retrieved from https://www.macdowellcolony.org/faqs.

MacKenzie, T. (2016). *Dive into inquiry*. Irvine, CA: Ed. Tech Team Press.

Maslow, A. H. (1970). *Motivation and personality*. New York: Harper & Row.

Maslow, A. H. (1971). *The farther reaches of human nature*. New York: The Viking Press.

Massachusetts Department of Elementary & Secondary Education. (2018). *Massachusetts state equity plan update 2018*. Malden, MA: Center for Instructional Support. Retrieved from http://www.doe.mass.edu/educators/equitableaccess/plan.html.

Ma, X., & Kishor, N. (1997). Assessing the relationship between attitude toward mathematics and achievement in mathematics: A meta-analysis. *Journal for Research in Mathematics Education*, *28*(1), 26. doi:10.2307/749662.

McClelland, C. (2018, August). The impact of artificial intelligence—widespread job losses. *IoT For All*. Retrieved from https://www.iotforall.com/impact-of-artificial-intelligence-job-losses/.

McLeod, D. (1992). Research on affect in mathematics education: A reconceptualization. In D. A. Grouws (ed.). *Handbook of research on mathematics teaching and learning* (pp. 575–96). New York: Macmillan.

Medina, J. (2008). *Brain rules: 12 principles for surviving and thriving at work, home, and school*. Seattle, WA: Pear Press.

Mehta, J., & Fine, S. (2019). *In search of deeper learning: The quest to remake the American high school*. Boston, MA: President and Fellows of Harvard College.

Merriam-Webster, Incorporated (2018). *The Merriam-Webster dictionary*. Martinsburg, WV: Merriam-Webster.

Miller, C. C. (2018, September 10). *Does teacher diversity matter in student learning?* Retrieved from https://www.nytimes.com/2018/09/10/upshot/teacher-diversity-effect-students-learning.html.

Mullis, I. V., Martin, M. O., Foy, P., & Arora, A. (2012). *TIMSS 2011 international results in mathematics*. Chestnut Hill, MA: International Association for the Evaluation of Educational Achievement. Retrieved from http://timssandpirls.bc.edu/timss2011/downloads/T11_IR_Mathematics_FullBook.pdf.

National Center of Children Living in Poverty. (2019). *Bank Street Graduate School of Education*. Retrieved from http://nccp.org/.

National Center for Education Statistics. (2015). *Percentage of high school dropouts among persons 16 to 24 years old (status dropout rate), by sex and race/ethnicity: Selected years, 1960 through 2014*. Retrieved from https://nces.ed.gov/programs/digest/d15/tables/dt15_219.70.asp.

National Center for Education Statistics. (2018). *Indicator 17: High school status dropout rates*. Retrieved from https://nces.ed.gov/programs/raceindicators/indicator_RDC.asp.

The National Commission on Excellence in Education. (1983, April). *A nation at risk: The imperative for educational reform*. A report to the nation and the secretary of education United States Department of Education. Retrieved from https://www.edreform.com/wp-content/uploads/2013/02/A_Nation_At_Risk_1983.pdf.

The Nation's Report Card. (n.d.). *NAEP data explorer* [data set]. September 27, 2019. Retrieved from https://www.nationsreportcard.gov/ndecore/landing.

New Hampshire Department of Education. (2010). *New Hampshire PreK–16 numeracy action plan for the 21st century*. Retrieved from *https://www.education.nh.gov/innovations/pre_k_num/documents/action_plan.pdf*.

Norton, M. (2012). *If you think money can't buy happiness, you're not spending it right* [Video file]. Retrieved from https://www.ted.com/talks/michael_norton_how_to_buy_happiness/up-next.

Novak, K. (2016). *UDL now! A teacher's guide to applying universal design for learning in today's classrooms* [Kindle Edition]. Wakefield, MA: CAST Professional Publishing.

Obama, M. (2015, June 20). *Remarks by the first lady at reach higher champions of change event*. Retrieved from https://obamawhitehouse.archives.gov/the-press-office/2015/06/30/remarks-first-lady-reach-higher-champions-change-event.

OECD. (2013). *PISA 2012 results: Ready to learn: Students' engagement, drive and self-beliefs (Volume III)*. PISA, OECD Publishing. Retrieved from http://dx.doi.org/10.1787/9789264201170-en.

Papert, S., & Harel, I. (1991). *Constructionism*. New York: Ablex Publishing Corporation. Retrieved from http://www.papert.org/articles/SituatingConstructionism.html.

Paulos, J. A. (1988). *Innumeracy: Mathematical illiteracy and its consequences*. New York: Hill and Wang.

Payne, R. K. (2005). *A framework for understanding poverty*. (4th Ed.). Highlands, TX: aha! Process, Inc.

Pierson, R. (2013). *Rita Pierson: Every kid needs a champion* [Video file]. Retrieved from http://www.ted.com/talks/rita_pierson_every_kid_needs_a_champion/transcript?language=en.

Pink, D. (2006). *A whole new mind: Why right-brainers will rule the future*. New York, NY: The Penguin Group.

Pink, D. H. (2012). *Drive: The surprising truth about what motivates us*. New York: Riverhead Books.

Preble, W. K., & Gordon, R. (2011). *Transforming school climate and learning: Beyond bullying and compliance*. Thousand Oaks, CA: Corwin.

Puntambekar, S., & Hübscher, R. (2005). Tools for scaffolding students in a complex learning environment: What have we gained and what have we missed? *Educational Psychologist, 40*(1), 1–12. Copyright © 2005, Lawrence Erlbaum Associates, Inc.

Putnam, R. D. (2016). *Our kids: The American dream in crisis*. New York: Simon & Schuster Paperbacks.

Quaglia, R. J. (2014). *Student voice: The instrument of change*. Thousand Oaks, CA: Corwin.

Quaglia, R. J. (2016). *School voice report*. Retrieved from http://quagliainstitute.org/dmsView/School_Voice_Report_2016.

Ramsey, L. (2017, February 22). *The "doomsday" vault that stores every known crop on the planet just got a delivery of nearly 50,000 seeds*. Retrieved from https://www.businessinsider.com/syrian-seeds-return-to-svalbard-doomsday-seed-vault-2017-2.

Rath, T. (2007). *StrengthsFinder 2.0*. New York: Gallup Press.

Ravitch, D. (2010). *The death and life of the great American school system: How testing and choice are undermining education*. New York: Basic Books.

Ravitch, D. (2014). *Reign of error: The hoax of the privatization movement and the danger to America's public schools*. New York: Vintage Books.

Ravitch, D. (2016). *The death and life of the great American school system: How testing and choice are undermining education*. New York: Basic Books.

Reynolds, M. (2017, July 26). *Donate your voice so Siri doesn't just work for white men*. Retrieved from https://www.newscientist.com/article/2141940-donate-your-voice-so-siri-doesnt-just-work-for-white-men/.

Robinson, K. (2010). *Bring on the learning revolution!* [Video file]. Retrieved from https://www.ted.com/talks/sir_ken_robinson_bring_on_the_revolution.

Robinson, K. (2017). *Out of our minds: The power of being creative*. (3rd Ed.). Chichester, UK: John Wiley & Sons, Incorporated.

Robinson, K., & Aronica, L. (2016). *Creative schools: The grassroots revolution that's transforming education*. New York: Penguin Books.

Robinson, K., & The RSA. (2010, October 14). *RSA Animates: Changing the educational paradigms* [Video file]. Retrieved from https://www.youtube.com/watch?v=zDZFcDGpL4U.

Romer, P. (2016). *Conditional optimism about progress and climate*. Retrieved from https://paulromer.net/conditional-optimism-about-progress-and-climate/.

Rose, T., & Ogas, O. (2018). *Dark horse: Achieving success through the pursuit of fulfilment*. New York: HarperOne.

Rotman, J. (n.d.). *New life project (AMATYC, et al.)* [Web blog post]. Retrieved from https://www.devmathrevival.net/?page_id=8.

Ruef, J. (2018, November 6). How to help students heal from "math trauma." *Education Week Teacher*. Retrieved from https://www.edweek.org/tm/articles/2018/11/06/how-to-help-students-heal-from-math.html?r=1182557424&mkey=B48EBDDE-F3E2-11E8-B662-C0C1C819EBCD.

Sagor, R. (1992). *How to conduct collaborative action research*. Alexandria, VA: Association for Supervision and Curriculum Development.

Sagor, R. (2000). *Guiding school improvement with action research*. Alexandria, VA: Association for Supervision and Curriculum Development.

Sagor, R. (2005). *The action research handbook: A four-step process for educators and school teams*. Thousand Oaks, CA: Corwin Press.

Schoenfeld, A. H. (1983). *Problem solving in the mathematics curriculum: A report, recommendations, and an annotated bibliography*. The Mathematical Association of America, Committee on the Undergraduate Program in Mathematics. Washington, DC: Mathematical Association of America.

Seidel, A. (2014). *The teacher dropout crisis*. Retrieved from https://www.npr.org/sections/ed/2014/07/18/332343240/the-teacher-dropout-crisis.

Selingo, J. J. (2017, April 7). *Why do colleges still give preference to children of alumni?* Retrieved from https://www.washingtonpost.com/news/grade-point/wp/2017/04/07/why-do-colleges-still-give-preference-to-children-of-alumni/.

Sousa, D. A. (2016). *Engaging the rewired brain*. West Palm Beach, FL: Learning Sciences International.

Sousa, D. A. (2017). *How the brain learns*. (5th Ed.). Thousand Oaks, CA: Corwin.

Spencer, J., & Juliani, A. (2016). *LAUNCH: Using design thinking to boost creativity and bring out the maker in every student*. San Diego, CA: Dave Burgess Consulting, Incorporated.

Steen, L.A. (ed.). (2001). *Mathematics and democracy: The case for quantitative literacy*. Princeton, NJ: National Council on Education and the Disciplines.

Steen, L. A. (2004). *Achieving quantitative literacy: An urgent challenge for higher education*. Washington, DC: Mathematical Association of America.

Strauss, V. (2017, September 15). *Of course algebra is important. It's also a huge problem* [Web blog post]. Retrieved from https://www.washingtonpost.com/news/answsheet/wp/2017/09/15/of-course-algebra-is-important-its-also-a-huge-problem/?noredirect=on&utm_term=.d6b7f57cba9f.

Strickland, E. (2009, January 12). *Attempt to control invasive species backfires spectacularly on an Antarctic island*. Retrieved from http://blogs.discovermagazine.com/80beats/2009/01/12/attempt-to-control-invasive-species-backfires-spectacularly-on-an-antarctic-island/#.XArVROS0WUk.

Sturgeon, N. (2019). *Why governments should prioritize well-being* [Video file]. Retrieved from https://www.ted.com/talks/nicola_sturgeon_why_governments_should_prioritize_well_being?language=en.

TeachThought Staff. (2017, November 14). *32 research-based instructional strategies*. Retrieved from https://www.teachthought.com/learning/32-research-based-instructional-strategies/.

Total Registration. (2017–2019). *2019 AP exam score distributions*. Retrieved from https://www.totalregistration.net/AP-Exam-Registration-Service/AP-Exam-Score-Distributions.php.

University of Oregon Center on Teaching and Learning. (2018). The dynamic indicators of basic early literacy skills (DIBELS, 8th ed.). University of Oregon DIBELS Data System. https://dibels.uoregon.edu/assessment/dibels/.

U.S. Department of Education. (2002). *No child left behind: A desktop reference*. Washington, DC: Office of Elementary and Secondary Education. Retrieved from https://www2.ed.gov/admins/lead/account/nclbreference/reference.pdf.

U.S. Department of Education. (2009). *Race to the top fund.* Retrieved from https://www2.ed.gov/programs/racetothetop/factsheet.html.

U.S. Department of Education. (2016). *The state of racial diversity in the educator workforce report.* Retrieved from https://www2.ed.gov/rschstat/eval/highered/racial-diversity/state-racial-diversity-workforce.pdf.

U.S. Department of Education. (2019, September). *Bridging the skills gap: Career and technical education in high school.* Retrieved from https://www2.ed.gov/datastory/cte/index.html.

Vandal, B. (2014). *Promoting gateway course success: Scaling corequisite academic support.* Retrieved from https://eric.ed.gov/?id=ED558791.

Vandal, B. (2017, June 18). *Scaling coreq for students who need additional academic support—chapter 2: Models that don't pass the coreq test* [Web blog post]. Retrieved from https://completecollege.org/article/scaling-coreq-for-students-who-need-additional-academic-support-chapter-2-models-that-dont-pass-the-coreq-test/.

Wagner, T. (2014). *The global achievement gap: Why even our best schools don't teach the new survival skills our children need and what we can do about it.* New York: Basic Books.

Wagner, T. (2016, August 9). *Tony Wagner 2016 Leadership Conference Speech.* Presented at the Fairfax County Public Schools Leadership Conference [Video file]. Retrieved from https://www.youtube.com/watch?v=QbaFyBFC6Jw&list=PLSz76NCRDYQGIC-imN_VkJXmMjSsyS5FF&index=4.

Wagner, T., & Compton, R. A. (2015). *Creating innovators: The making of young people who will change the world.* New York: Scribner.

Wagner, T., & Dintersmith, T. (2016). *Most likely to succeed: Preparing our kids for the innovation era.* New York: Scribner.

Webb, N. L. (2002). *Depth-of-knowledge levels for four content areas.* Retrieved from http://facstaff.wcer.wisc.edu/normw/All%20content%20areas%20%20DOK%20levels%2032802.pdf

Wiggins, G., & McTighe. (2005). *Understanding by design* (expanded 2nd Ed.). Alexandria, VA: Association for Supervision and Curriculum Development.

Wilkins, J. L., & Ma, X. (2003). Modeling change in student attitude toward and beliefs about mathematics. *The Journal of Educational Research, 97*(1), 52–63. doi:10.1080/00220670309596628.

World Economic Forum. (2016). *The global competitiveness report 2016–2017.* Geneva, Switzerland: World Economic Forum.

Zhao, Y. (2009). *Catching up or leading the way: American education in the age of globalization.* Alexandria, VA: Association for Supervision and Curriculum Development.

Zhao, Y. (2012). *World class learners: Educating creative and entrepreneurial students.* Thousand Oaks, CA: Corwin.

About the Authors

Richard A. Andrusiak is a mathematics professor and department chair at River Valley Community College in Claremont, New Hampshire. He is certified as an elementary mathematics specialist, upper level mathematics educator (pre-algebra to AP mathematics), and curriculum coordinator. His work and research in mathematics education focuses on curriculum development, students' attitudes toward mathematics, and equity and access issues. He is a former New Hampshire State Supervisor of K–12 mathematics, where he worked with professors, public school teachers, and other mathematics specialists around the nation on improving mathematics education.

Amanda Bastoni is an award-winning author, grant writer, educational leader, and Career and Technical Education (CTE) director in the Nashua School District, New Hampshire. She is certified as a CTE teacher, principal, vice principal, and CTE director. She has developed new pathways and programs targeted to meet the needs of English Language Learners and nontraditional students, created interdisciplinary courses, organized fundraising campaigns, developed educational publicity programs, and written educational articles for local and national outlets. In 2019, she was named New Hampshire CTE State Leader of the Year.

Carlton J. Fitzgerald has been an educator since 1971. He was a classroom teacher for twelve years, working mostly with reluctant or struggling students. He was a public school administrator for twenty-four years, working at all levels for his school district. In 2007, he began his full-time work at New England College, where he served as an associate professor of education, director of the MED program, and associate dean of education. Currently, he is retired from full-time work and lives in Romania, serving as an adjunct faculty member both at NEC and the University of Oradea (Romania).

Christopher Geraghty is a social studies educator and department chair at Kearsarge Regional High School located in North Sutton, New Hampshire. He is certified as a 5–12 social studies educator and a school principal by the state of New Hampshire. He also serves as a social studies instructional coach for the Center for Secondary School Redesign, and guest lecturer at New England College, teaching graduate courses with a focus on inquiry-based education and the integration of STEAM across the curriculum.

Simona Laurian-Fitzgerald is an associate professor at the University of Oradea (Romania). Her specialty areas include children's literature, education, and English. Prior to her work at the university, she was an elementary teacher for five years. Her research interests include cooperative learning and other student-centered teaching and learning strategies. She has experience working with students online, in hybrid classes, as well as her face-to-face classes. She also works with teachers to help them develop their skills for advancement in their careers.

Ruthann Petruno-Goguen is currently the superintendent of schools for the Webster Public Schools—a "turnaround" district in Massachusetts. She is an experienced educator and change-agent, with over twenty years of experience serving children and teachers in rural, urban, and suburban school districts.

www.ingramcontent.com/pod-product-compliance
Lightning Source LLC
Chambersburg PA
CBHW051812230426
43672CB00012B/2704